AUSTRALIAN
PHRASEBOOK

Denise Angelo, Carolyn Coleman &
Melanie Wilkinson
Peter Austin & Barry Blake
Susan Butler, Mark Newbrook & Jane Curtain
Alan Dench
Institute for Aboriginal Development
Dana Ober

Australian Phrasebook
2nd edition

Published by
    Lonely Planet Publications
    Head Office: PO Box 617, Hawthorn, Vic 3122, Australia
    Branches: 150 Linden Street, Oakland CA 94607, USA
                10a Spring Place, London NW5 3BH, UK
                1 rue du Dahomey, 75011 Paris, France

Printed by
Colorcraft Ltd, Hong Kong

Cover Illustration
    'What can I 'roo for you, mate?' by Penelope Richardson

Published
    November 1998

National Library of Australia Cataloguing in Publication Data

    Australian phrasebook
    2nd edition
    Includes index.
    ISBN 0 86442 576 7.

© Lonely Planet Publications Pty Ltd, 1998
Stori ba Hanting gada Biliken © Maureen Hodgson 1998
Central Australian Chapter © Language Centre, Institute for
Aboriginal Development 1998
Cover Illustration © Lonely Planet

About the Authors

The Australian English section of this book was written by Susan Butler, Publisher of the *Macquarie Dictionary*, with additional contributions from Mark Newbrook and Jane Curtain, Department of Linguistics, Monash University. Richard Plunkett wrote the wine and beer sections and contributed to the chapter on sport; and Carolyn Papworth wrote the Introduction to the Food chapter and the sections on Nightlife and Café Society. Thanks to Surf Lifesaving Australia for their assistance.

The Central Australian Aboriginal Languages chapter was compiled by Jenny Tindale from the Institute for Aboriginal Development, with contributions from Lizzie Ellis, Gavan Breen and Robert Hoogenraad, and ideas and assistance from Lorna Wilson, Mark MacLean and Ken Grime.

The Top End Aboriginal Languages chapter was written by Denise Angelo from Diwurruwurru-jaru Aboriginal Corporation together with Carolyn Coleman and Melanie Wilkinson, both linguists with the Northern Territory Education Department. Thanks to Maureen Hodgson who provided the Kriol text *Stori ba Hanting gada Biliken*; and also Murray Garde and Kuninjku speakers of the Maningrida area for help with Kuninjku examples. Many people, including Brett Baker, Erika Charola, Ian Green, Mark Harvey, Frances Kofod, Francesca Merlan, Jen Munro and Nick Reid assisted with checking the language maps.

The Western Australian Aboriginal Languages chapter was written by Alan Dench of the Centre of Linguistics, University of Western Australia. Barry Blake and Peter Austin wrote the chapter on the Aboriginal Languages of Victoria and New South Wales, and Barry Blake put together the Introductory chapter, with contributions from Denise Angelo and Jenny Tindale.

Dana Ober wrote the chapter on the Languages of Torres Strait. Thanks to Anima Ghee, Bakoi Pilot and Puitam Wees for contributions on their languages.

From the Publisher

This book came to fruition thanks to a great team of happy little Vegemites. It was edited by Elizabeth Swan between her gruelling training sessions for the Seed Spitting Contest at the Coominya Grape Festival. Sally Steward proofread the book and watched over production with the keen eye of a maggie. Penelope Richardson wove her magic on the book's design and layout, as well as the ripper illustrations and bonzer cover. Peter D'Onghia proofread the book, did the contents and index, and was most generous indeed with his supply of Pez and golden chalices. Fabrice Rocher proofread the layout design and has now decided to change his name to Fazza. Hats off and thanks to Paul Clifton and Piotr Czajkowski for their work on the beaut maps throughout the book.

The languages in this book are the indigenous Australian languages, and English, the language commonly spoken by all Australians. As Australia is a multicultural country, there are also many community languages, which we have not been able to include, but we acknowledge their contribution to Australian culture.

All the language maps in this book show approximate locations only.

CONTENTS

AUSTRALIAN ENGLISH

INTRODUCTION

HISTORY

Australian English is a variety of English with a very interesting
and colourful history. When the British Government established
a convict settlement in Sydney in 1788 they weren't aware of the
linguistic consequences. The history of Australian English is one
of transplantation (the language was transported from the UK
to Australia) and adaptation (English underwent changes to ac-
commodate the majority of the speakers, namely the convicts).
As time went by, both the convicts and the free settlers took
English and adapted it to their new home, by twisting meanings
of existing words or borrowing new ones to suit.

Convict Influence

The earliest Australian English was very much a 'working class'
variety as the vast majority of the arrivals (mostly convicts) were
poor, and for the most part, unskilled. Some words have filtered
through from what was called the 'Flash Language' – the thieves'
language of London – which earned respectability on Australian
shores. In London a 'plant' was the name for stolen goods hidden away to be collected later when the coast was clear. In early
Australian English the word 'plant' came to refer to stores and
provisions hidden away in the bush to be collected on a return
trip; to 'plant' something was to put it away safely for later. When
contemporary Australians speak of 'planting' the Christmas
presents where the children can't find them, they're demonstrat-
ing the influence of earlier British criminal slang on the Australian English vocabulary.

Early British English Influence

Words and expressions of British English took on a whole new
meaning in the colonial circumstances of Australia. In the UK a
'paddock' is a small enclosed meadow. In Australia a 'paddock'
may extend further than the eye can see. In the UK a 'creek' is a

small tidal inlet. In Australia a 'creek' is a subsidiary of a river, which can be bigger than the Thames.

Australian English is predominantly a town-based variety as most of the convicts and early settlers were from British towns and cities, especially London and the south-east of England. This partially explains why the British English names for features of the countryside such as 'brook', 'glen' and 'dale' haven't really become part of the general Australian English vocabulary.

Early Irish English Influence

The other main regional influence on Australian English was that of Irish English, as convicts were also transported from Ireland following the 1798 Irish rebellion. Later on, many Irish migrants were also forced to settle in Australia after the Irish famine of the 1840s. Australian English has therefore incorporated several Irish English words and phrases into its general vocabulary. The term sheila, for example, is an Irish girl's name which was used in early Australian English to apply to any Irish girl, just as Paddy was used for any Irish man. Later on sheila was used for all women alike, although it's not a term which women necessarily apply to themselves. In colloquial Australian English, this term can also be used as a derogatory label for a man believed to 'behave' like a woman. Irish English has also had some influence on Australian English grammar (see page 17).

Incorporating Aboriginal Words

In order to meet the needs of the settlers in a new and unexplored environment many words were borrowed into early Australian English from the Aboriginal languages. These words were particularly used for describing and labelling the unfamiliar flora and fauna. Animals were named this way: the kangaroo, koala, wallaby, wombat and dingo. Some indigenous plants are the mallee, the jarrah and the coolibah. Birds include the kookaburra, the currawong and the budgerigar; fish include the barramundi, the wobbegong and the yabby, and among the reptiles are the perentie and the taipan. Some features of the environment are the billabong ('waterhole'), the bombora ('treacherous current over submerged rock') and the willy-willy ('sudden twisting gust of wind'). Typically Aboriginal tools and instruments include the boomerang ('curved piece of hard wood used as returning missile') and the didgeridoo ('long wooden musical wind instrument').

The Goldfields

The growth of the goldfields in the 1850s brought an influx of people from all over the world, including the UK, Ireland, Europe, North America and Asia. Many British and American slang and colloquial expressions emerged in Australia during this period. There are some words which have survived from the diggings; words like fossick which meant 'dig through heap of dirt for any leftover gold', and which now means 'go carefully through anything in order to find something'. The word digger, brought to Australia via America during the gold rushes, referred at this stage to a miner, and since miners for very practical reasons always worked in pairs, the digger became the symbol of mateship in Australia, particularly in the emotional climate of WWI.

Early 20th Century Australian English

The Federation of the Australian States, which was formed on 1 January 1901, was a watershed in Australian history and separates the former colonial society from the modern nation. There have been a number of significant milestones passed in this century which have all left their mark on Australian English.

In WWI, soldiers contributed some slang to Australian English, such as furphy ('rumour'). During the war water was supplied to the soldiers in water carts made by John Furphy. The obvious place for the soldiers to exchange information of doubtful value was at the water cart, so these rumours came to be called furphies.

During the Great Depression the figure who emerged was the battler ('person who struggled against all odds'). The battler was usually surviving on the susso ('sustenance payments'). These days you'll often hear the phrase 'little Aussie battler', referring to a character-type almost revered in Australia.

WWII brought an influx of Americanisms, both during and after it. But Australian army talk also included words like troppo ('mad from spending too much time in the tropics') and spinebashing ('resting').

CONTEMPORARY AUSTRALIAN ENGLISH

The 20th century pattern of Australian English, particularly since WWII, is clearly one of American English influence. Although Australia's English-speaking immigrants have mainly come from the UK, the ever-increasing contact with the USA through military activity, tourism and the media has led to a noticeable Americanisation of Australian English. Australian children appear to be still resisting using 'cookie' in favour of the Australian 'biscuit', and pronounce the name of the letter 'z' to rhyme with 'head' rather than with 'bee'; but they readily refer to other people as 'guys' and 'dudes' without any strong feeling that these words are American.

Other currents that might be noticed in today's Australian English are the differences between the language of the older generation and of the younger generation, and between that of the people who live in the city and of those who live in the bush ('country'). Much of the colloquial language, in particular, that's regarded as distinctively Australian, might not be so popular with the younger generation living in the cities, who tend to take their fashionable colloquialisms from America.

Migrant English

Australia has a significant number of people with migrant backgrounds, most of whom speak other languages in the home. Naturally their English is influenced to some extent by their other languages and it's common to hear people described as 'sounding Greek' or whatever. Maybe over the years some of these features will spread to the wider population. People of British background are often not included under the heading of migrants because they're native speakers of English.

PRONUNCIATION

INTRODUCTION

Very early in the days of colonial settlement British visitors commented, usually disparagingly, on the Australian accent. Various attempts were made to correct the so-called 'twisted vowels' and 'barbaric noises' made by the locals from that early point in colonial history until comparatively recently. But the accent that formed among the children of the convicts has proved remarkably resistant to such efforts.

THE MELTING POT THEORY

The convict settlement included speakers of various British dialects whose accents remained much as they were when they landed on Australian shores. Being transported didn't change a Yorkshireman from being a Yorkshireman, and there was no way that a Cockney convict was going to start sounding like his military masters. But the children of the convicts were like children anywhere – desperate to conform, desperate to win the acceptance of the other children. So with no one particular local form of language to guide them, they forged a new accent of their own, taking features from the various accents represented among them.

THE STRANDED DIALECT THEORY

The melting pot theory does seem to have a lot going for it, but there's an alternative theory to account for the Australian accent. This goes along the lines that there was a predominant dialect among the convict community, but this dialect is difficult to trace back to its British origins for two reasons. One reason is that while there's a conservative force operating in a colony that resists change, that force doesn't operate back in the mother country, where the dialect continues to change, leaving its older form stranded in the colony.

The other factor which obscures identification is that some changes are forced on the colonial speakers by circumstances. The presence of one strongly represented accent might bring about a number of changes simply through the pressure of the number of its speakers. This can confuse the issue, making it harder to decide just what the original home accent was, particularly when that accent itself has also adapted in various ways back in the UK. A sensible compromise might involve the view that both theories are partly valid.

PRONUNCIATION

BATMANIA

Rumour has it that Melbourne narrowly escaped being named 'Batmania' in honour of John Batman who selected the city's site in 1835. But even without 'Batmania' on the map, Australia still has its fair share of towns and geographical features with interesting names, that have us all wondering how and why.

Bald Head (WA)
Banana (Qld)
Big Billy Bore (Vic)
Booby Island (Qld)
Broken Bucket
    Reserve (Vic)
Butty Head (WA)
Cape Liptrap (Vic)
Hat Head (NSW)

Indented Head (Vic)
Lake Disappointment (WA)
Mexican Hat Beach (WA)
Mt Hopeless (SA)
Nightcap (NSW)
One Arm Point (Vic)
Salmon Gums (WA)
Snug (Tas)
Turtle Head (Qld)

INFLUENCE OF AMERICAN ENGLISH PRONUNCIATION

Despite the obvious influence of American English on Australian English vocabulary (and some grammatical features) in recent times, the only area of activity where Australians actually sound American is in popular song. Australian pop singers tend to regularly use a pseudo-American accent in song but an Australian accent in their everyday speech. This tendency is shared by pop singers from other English-speaking communities, who also sound American only when singing. Outside pop music, Australians don't pronounce words like 'nuclear' or 'tomato' in the characteristically American way, or pronounce the final '-r' in words like 'car'. Very few words show any American influence on their pronunciation.

PRONUNCIATION ACROSS AUSTRALIA

Australian English is remarkably homogeneous even though the enormous distance from the west coast to the east coast is in excess of 3000km. Despite the size of Australia, most speakers apparently sound the same or very similar, particularly when compared to the differences observed in the UK or the USA. In fact the main geographical differences in pronunciation in Australian English are thought to be urban versus rural differences, the rural accent supposedly being slower and broader than the urban. For this reason, many people claim that accent variability in Australia is social and stylistic rather than geographical.

WAGGA WAGGA

The country town of Wagga Wagga in NSW is pronounced 'wogga wogga' but like most Australians, feel free to call it just plain 'wogga'.

There is, however, considerable evidence that subtle differences in Australian English pronunciation between geographical regions not only exist but are becoming more noticeable. Many speakers in Melbourne, Brisbane and Hobart, use the short 'a' vowel (as in 'cat') in words like 'castle', 'graph' and 'dance', where the long 'a' vowel (as in 'cart') is normally used by speakers from some other parts of Australia in these words, especially the first two.

Similarly, in South Australia and parts of Victoria the word 'school' and others like it are pronounced with a clipped, shortened vowel that many other Australians don't produce.

One distinctive pattern that has emerged among the younger generation is the use of a rising intonation. Some statements, such as 'It's a lovely day' often now end in the kind of rising intonation which is usually reserved for questions.

There aren't very many grammatical features exclusive to Australian English and the ones that exist seldom cause any confusion, but they may surprise some visitors.

- **all/both ... not**
  When young Australians say things like 'All those letters didn't arrive', they usually mean 'None of those letters arrived'. Older Australians (like many people in other English-speaking countries) don't often use such sentences, but if they do they put the stress on 'all' and the sentence then means 'Some of them arrived and some didn't'. And some people use such sentences in both ways!

- **verbs with names of teams**
  In Australia, the names of teams can be either singular or plural: so people and the media may say either 'Collingwood (the football team) is doing well' or 'Collingwood are doing well'. In the UK team names are always plural ('Liverpool are doing well'); the American usage is more like the Australian. Although less common, Australians also use singular nouns and pronouns to refer to teams, which Americans often avoid. So in an Australian press report a sentence like 'It's the reigning champion' could be about a football team.

- **my same, etc**
  Some Australians say things like 'Can I keep my same phone number if I change address?' In most other English-speaking countries the expression in such cases is always 'the same'.

- **mustn't**
  This feature of Australian English comes from Irish English and is therefore shared with some parts of England. Many Australians say things like 'She mustn't be in; the lights are all out.' In most other English-speaking countries people would say 'She can't be in' or, in the USA, 'She must not be in.'

- **usedn't to**

  For most English speakers, the negative of 'used to' is now 'didn't use to', as in 'I didn't use to like beer but now I do'. The older form 'usedn't to' ('I usedn't to like beer …') is now rare, but it survives best in Australia.

- **conditionals**

  If an Australian says something like 'If that happened …' it doesn't necessarily mean that they think the event in question might happen (but probably will not) in the future, as in 'If that happened tomorrow I'd be surprised'. It sometimes means that it *could* have happened in the past but did not, as in 'If that happened yesterday I'd have been surprised'. Most people from other English-speaking countries would say 'If that had happened …' or, in the USA, 'If that would have happened …'.

HAVE A GANDER …

… doesn't mean to eat a goose, it means to 'look at' and so do these:

bo-peep
  'Take a bo-peep at that bloke.'

geezer
  'Eh, have a geezer at that this.'

perve
  to look at in a lustful manner

squizz
  'Hey, cop a squizz at this!'

sticky beak
  to look, usually uninvited, as in 'I had a sticky beak at the neighbour's new pool when they were out'

RHYMING SLANG

after darks	sharks
aristotle/arra	bottle
Bob Hope	soap/dope (marijuana)
comic-cuts	guts
cheese and kisses	missus (wife)
dead horse	sauce, usually tomato sauce
hey-diddle-diddle	piddle
hit-and-miss	piss
Jimmy Britts	shits
Jimmy Dancer	cancer
Joe Blake	snake
Richard the Third	turd
steak and kidney	Sydney
tom(my) tits	shits

- **may & might**

  If an Australian says something like 'This may have happened ...', the event referred to may sometimes be one that *could* have happened but did not. Elsewhere the speaker would normally mean that they don't know whether it happened or not, which is also a possible meaning in Australia.

  For the former meaning most non-Australians would use 'might', not 'may'. Australians often say things like 'Mandy said that this may happen ...', even where the event predicted by Mandy would now be in the past if it did happen; again, 'might' would be more usual elsewhere.

- **different to**

  Most Australians use 'to' after 'different', as in 'Adelaide is very different to Perth'. But some older people and most formal texts prefer the more typically British word 'from', and the originally American English form 'than' is increasingly popular.

- **irregardless**
  This word is a blend of 'irrespective' and 'regardless' and has the same meaning ('Irregardless of what you think, I'm going to do it!'). It's heard elsewhere but seems to be especially common in Australia.

- **hottest, highest, etc.**
  When an Australian news report says that yesterday was the hottest May day since 1927, it doesn't imply – as it might elsewhere – that the day in May 1927 was even hotter; it implies that the earlier temperature was lower. This can be very confusing at first, especially for people who read lots of weather or sport reports.

- **as well …**
  Like Canadians (but not like most Americans, or British people), Australians sometimes begin sentences with 'As well …' (not 'As well as …', which is normal everywhere), as in 'As well, there are three other problems'.

- **as such …**
  Young Australians often use 'As such …' in cases where 'So …', 'Therefore …' or some other similar expression would be usual elsewhere: 'The building's locked; as such, we can't get our things'.

- **youse**
  Pronounced 'yooze', this has become the plural of 'you'. You may hear sentences like 'Where are youse going?'. Only used by the grammatically challenged!

GENERAL AUSSIE ENGLISH

AUSSIE INFORMALITY

Most of the very first English-speaking settlers in Australia were convicted criminals, which may account for slang and colloquial language becoming a normal part of Australian English. Being informal and speaking informally is very important in Australia – arguably more so than in other areas of the world – though this shouldn't be overstated as Australians can also be just as formal as anyone else when they think this is important. For many Australians, being informal increases the desirable attributes of mateship, equality, solidarity and colonial escapism from a class-ridden society. Although Australians often portray their country as classless, this is again something of an exaggeration, though perhaps fair in terms of contrast with the UK.

It is also said of Australian English that it has a wide range of inventive, colourful slang and colloquialisms. It is perhaps truer to say that the range of colloquialisms is much the same as in any other language but that Australians make more of it. Indeed many seem to flaunt it.

LANGUAGE DIFFICULTIES

If you're visiting Australia, and particularly if you're not from an English-speaking background, you must quickly learn to communicate in a predominantly monolingual English-speaking society. You must also contend with a society which tends to use much informal language in its variety of English. It's not surprising that some of the colloquial expressions cause much confusion for those visitors who haven't encountered them before.

As a visitor, you may be puzzled why a red-headed person is nicknamed **Blue** or **Bluey**, particularly as red and blue are distinctly different colours. You also have to deal with **blue** being used in other, unrelated contexts such as **feeling blue** meaning 'feeling depressed', **making a blue** meaning 'making a mistake', **picking a blue** meaning 'starting a fight or argument', **copping a** bluey meaning 'receiving a traffic infringement notice', watching a blue movie meaning 'watching a pornographic film' and the boys in blue meaning 'the police'.

You may also experience difficulty with the many meanings associated with the word crook, such as feeling crook meaning 'feeling sick', eating something crook meaning 'eating something contaminated and likely to cause food poisoning', being crook at/with someone meaning 'being angry with them', being a crook meaning 'being a dishonest person such as a swindler or a thief', and something being crook meaning 'something being illegal or broken'.

MEETING PEOPLE

Australians are known for their easy-going informality and friendliness. However it always helps to have a few of the basics of any language and the obvious starting point is how to say hello. G'day is the truly established Australian greeting but there are a few variations on this theme. This needs to be followed up with the appropriate goodbye.

Greetings

G'day.
Hi; Hiya!
How ya goin' mate – orright?   (older generation – often male)
How's tricks?
How are ya?

Farewells

Catch-you-later; Cop-you-later.
Ciao.
Hoo-roo. (old-fashioned)
See you (later); See ya (later).

To express appreciation, bonzer, ripper or bewdy will do fine. No worries is a popular Australian response akin to 'no problems', 'that's OK', 'sure thing'.

RHYMING SLANG

Rhyming slang in Australia is an inheritance from London English, particularly Cockney. Some of it was brought over from England, and some was developed within Australia. There are many Australians who seem to enjoy using rhyming slang, but the community as a whole operates successfully without it, apart from the odd fragments which have become embedded in the language.

babbler	*babbling brook*	cook
bone	*dog and bone*	phone
captain	*Captain Cook*	look
hammer	*hammer and tack*	back
molly	*molly the monk*	drunk
Noah	*Noah's ark*	shark
on one's pat	*on one's Pat Malone*	alone
optic	*optic nerve*	perve/look

barmaid's blush *a flush (in poker)*
it also refers to a drink made from port wine and lemonade, or rum and raspberry

amster *Amsterdam ram*
an old-fashioned word for a person who tries to drum up business outside a sideshow. 'Amsterdam ram' is a British word for the same kind of showman, also known as a spruiker, urger or drummer.

butcher's *butcher's hook*
a look, as in 'Have a butcher's at this'. Don't confuse this with the following:

butcher's *butcher's hook*
crook; feeling sick. When you have the lurgi (some vague unidentifiable illness, usually one that's going around), then you 'feel butcher's'.

RHYMING SLANG

china *China plate – mate*
an old-fashioned word for a friend

Dad & Dave
shave. Dad & Dave were characters in a pre-WWII radio show.

frog and toad
road, as in 'Let's hit the frog 'n' toad!'

loaf *loaf of bread*
head. 'Use your loaf' is an encouragement to think rather than to cut some sandwiches.

onka *onkaparinga*
finger. Onkaparinga's the name of a kind of woollen rug.

pommy *pomegranate – immigrant*
a person of British nationality and usually Anglo-Celtic extraction. Often shortened to Pom.

reginalds *Reg Grundies*
undies/underwear. Reg Grundy is a well-known TV entrepreneur. Also known as reggies

scarper *Scapa Flow – go*
go away, usually at high speed or with some urgency

septic *septic tank – Yank*
an American. Also shortened to seppo

titfer *tit for tat*
hat. Another term for hat is this-an'-that

warwicks *Warwick Farm*
arms. Named after a well-known racecourse in Sydney.

COLLOQUIAL EXPRESSIONS
Verb Phrases

a wake-up	be aware of something, as in 'He's a wake-up to it' meaning 'he's aware of it'
bludge	laze around and evade responsibilities
bung	put, as in 'Just bung it in the oven'
bored shitless	be extremely bored
cark it	collapse/die
chuck a berko	express extreme anger
clobber	hit
come a cropper/ gutser	fall over, to have an accident or to not succeed
crack onto	chat up someone
dip one's lid	show respect for someone, or something worthy of attention
fartarse around	waste time
feel like a shag on a rock	feel alone, deserted, forlorn, left out
get a guernsey	succeed or win approval; originally to be selected for a football team
get stuck into somebody	argue strongly; berate somebody
give a bumsteer	mislead
hang out for	be in a state of anticipation
have tickets on oneself	have an inflated opinion of one's worth
in the raw/nuddy	be naked
lash at it	try
live on the smell of an oily rag	live frugally
pash (on)	kiss passionately
pick the eyes out of it	take all the best bits
play funny buggers	behave in a foolish way or in a deceitful manner
pull a swiftie	take part in a deceitful or unfair act
pull one's head in	mind one's own business
rapt	very keen about something or someone; derived from 'enraptured'

see a man about a dog	do something secretively; usually refers to going to the toilet (mainly used by men)
shoot through	leave (quickly); to die
to have a shot at it	try
shout	buy a round of drinks in a pub
skite	boast
spill one's guts	reveal a secret or a complicated and interesting story
stick your bib in	interfere, as in 'Who asked you to stick your bib in?'
stir the possum	tease and/or deliberately cause trouble
strike a blow	help with housework, etc
swing the billy	put the kettle on with the intention of making a cup of tea
tee-up	arrange an appointment
wag	be absent from school without permission

Describing People

ankle biter; rug-rat; tacker	child
blue heeler	policeman
checkout chick	supermarket checkout clerk
cobber	friend
curly	nickname for a bald person
joe blow/bloggs	the average citizen, any man
larrikin	mischievous young person
mate	friend
mate's rates	a discount rate for a friend
micks	Catholics
old cheese	mother
poofter	homosexual male
quack	doctor/medical practitioner
rooted/zonked	exhausted
shark biscuits	novice surfers
starkers	nude
tightarse	a stingy person
wanker/tosser	idiot and/or pretentious person

bloke
    adult male person. Shared with British usage, but
    increasingly replaced by the American form 'guy' for
    younger speakers, although 'guy' is used by some people to
    include females.
bludger
    person who does no or very little work
bogan
    person, usually from a very working class urban area, who
    dresses in tight jeans, tight jumpers and moccasins (modern
    usage)
born in a tent
    with a tendency to leave the door open
couldn't organise a pissup in a brewery
    refers to a very disorganised person
flash as a rat with a gold tooth
    someone that considers themselves very fancy
fruit loop
    term for a foolish or crazy person
hoon
    foolhardy youth who drives fast and recklessly
lower than a snake's belly/armpits
    very mean, cruel or dishonest
more comebacks than Dame Nellie Melba
    said of someone who keeps coming back for more (Dame
    Nellie Melba was a world-famous opera singer who had
    several official farewells, and just as many comebacks)
no flies on him/her
    clever, alert and can't easily be fooled
no-hoper/loser
    person who displays great incompetence
not know somebody from a bar of soap
    to be totally unfamiliar with somebody
old boiler
    elderly woman (from 'boiling chickens')
rough as guts
    very rough, rowdy, untidy, distasteful

shit kicker
> the person who does all the menial or unpopular jobs at
> work or home

spunk
> good-looking person of either sex, as in 'What a spunk!';
> similarly spunk-rat, though usually used to describe a male

wouldn't shout if a shark bit her
> said of a person who's stingy or unduly frugal and won't
> buy drinks for others

Describing Places & Objects

all the go	fashionable
as scarce as hen's teeth	very rare
as useful as a glass door on a dunny	extremely useless
big smoke	city
blower/rap-rod	telephone
cheap as chips	very cheap
cop shop	police station

DID YOU KNOW ...

Mt Kosciusko is Australia's highest peak at 2228m and was named in honour of a Polish hero of the American War of Independence.

Apparently the mountain's name is one big spelling mistake with a 'z' missing before the final 'k', but however it's spelt, you can confidently pronounce it as 'kozzi-osko'.

cruddy	of poor quality
idiot box	TV
on the nose	very smelly
o.s.	overseas
poo tickets	toilet paper
pong	bad smell
shrapnel	the leftover coins
stormstick	umbrella
thunderbox	toilet
tuckshop	canteen; kiosk at a school
wonky	unstable/unsteady

boomerang
    something which must be returned. 'This book is a boo-
    merang' means 'Please return it when you've finished
    reading it'.
chockers
    completely full, from 'chock-a-block'
Honkers
    Hong Kong. 'You'd be bonkers not to go via Honkers' was
    an advertising phrase encouraging Australians to have a
    holiday stopover in Hong Kong.
more of something than one could poke a stick at
    a very great deal of something
not worth a crumpet; a brass razoo
    not worth anything

Describing Actions & Situations

dead cert/set	absolutely certain
flat chat/out	doing something very quickly
hang on a tick/sec	wait a moment
piece of piss	easy task
pocket billiards	male adjusting his genitals
prang/bingle	car accident
rattle your dags;	hurry up!
get a wriggle on!	
reckon!	you bet!

GENERAL AUSSIE ENGLISH

rug up	dress warmly
r.s.	lousy (ratshit)
send her down, Hughie	let it rain, please God!
she'll be apples; she's sweet	everything will be OK
stinker	a very hot day
too right!	yes, most definitely, of course

two shakes of a lamb's tail
  very short amount of
  time
crust
  job; way of earning a
  living, as in 'What do
  you do for a crust?'
fizzer
  a failure; disappoint-
  ment, as in 'The party
  was a real fizzer'.
flat out like a lizard
drinking
  be very busy
go mad and be shot
  be out of sight or
  disappear, usually used
  in response to chil-
  dren's incessant queries
  about the whereabouts
  of someone
great Aussie salute
  waving arm motion of
  an Australian which is
  used to brush flies away from the face
not even in the race for it
  having no hope of achieving a goal
not know somebody from a bar of soap
  be totally unfamiliar with somebody
Rafferty's rules
  no rules at all, very unorganised
ron
  later; contraction of later on, as in 'I'll take this for ron'
spewing
  very upset, as in 'She was spewing about that'; or as a
  reaction to disappointing news – 'Oh no, spewin'!' Also a
  popular term for vomiting.

TALK TOO MUCH

Aussies have many terms to
describe incessant talk.

  yapping
  yacking
  verbal diarrhoea
  raving on
  chew someone's ear off
  flap the gums

talk someone blind
  bore someone by
  talking on and on …

ear bash
  constant, often berating
  talk

---

wog
> virus or stomach upset (older usage); person of or thought
> to be of Mediterranean or Middle Eastern extraction
> (generally quite a derogatory expression)

yakka
> hard, strenuous work (from an Aboriginal language)

yonks
> a long time. 'I haven't seen Thommo for yonks'

'Like a ...'

The little expression like a ... opens a world of possibilities in the
Australian context. Some of the more well-known or remarkable comparisons are as follows:

like a cocky on a biscuit tin
> left out, not included; used after Arnotts chose to use a
> colourful parrot rather than a sulphur crested cockatoo as
> part of their logo

like a cut snake
> in an angry fashion

like a dunny in a desert
> standing out, being very conspicuous

like a moll at a christening
> extremely out of place and uncomfortable

like a rat up a drain pipe
> very quick, restless and erratic

like a rooster one day and a feather duster the next
> very important, special and useful one moment and very
> unimportant and common the next

like a stunned mullet
> refers to a person in complete bewilderment, astonishment
> or a state of inertia. The mullet, being a large fish, is knocked
> over the head after it's been caught, and as it's a common fish
> to catch, perhaps its dazed expression has become familiar.

'... like a'

charge like a wounded bull
  to charge outrageously high prices
feel like a grease spot
  feel hot and sweaty, about to dissolve into a pool of grease
go down like a lead balloon
  be a complete failure
go through like a dose of salts
  if something goes through you like a dose of salts, it has the
  same effect as a laxative; but if a person goes through you
  like a dose of salts, they've just been very angry with you
looks like a dog's breakfast
  refers to anything in a dreadful mess
need (something) like a hole in the head
  an ironic statement, for obvious reasons
running around like a chook with its head cut off
  making a lot of commotion but not getting anywhere. This
  is the ultimate in pointless activity! The image goes back to
  the scene by the chopping block where the chook (chicken)
  which has been selected for dinner gets its head cut off.
  There's a moment when the headless chook keeps running
  around until the message finally gets through to its body.

DID YOU KNOW ...

The charming Australian word dunny ('toilet') that colours so many phrases – all alone like a country dunny, as cunning as a dunny rat and dunny paper – is a diminutive form of 'dunnaken', a term borrowed from an English dialect with a literal meaning of 'dung-house'.

GENERAL AUSSIE ENGLISH

'Short of a ...'

Australians often use expressions using 'short of a ...' forms to describe someone who appears stupid or who displays low intelligence. It's not uncommon to hear expressions like: He's a ... short of a ...

a book short of a library	a penny short of a pound
a can short of a slab	a sandwich short of a picnic
an egg short of a dozen	a snag short of a barbie
a grape short of a bunch	a stubby short of a six pack

SHORTENED FORMS

Australians are fond of cutting their words down to size, usually by taking the first part of the word and finishing it off at an appropriate point with -ie or -o. This can be just for the sake of general efficiency (why say 'communist' when you could say commie?) or to indicate affection (children can be referred to as the kiddies, or even more playfully, the kiddie-winks). The -ie ending can be used to create a useful noun where no noun existed before, from an adjective. Thus from 'green' we get the greenie ('person concerned with the environment'). The -o ending is more neutral than the -ie one, and can be used to convey a certain nonchalance. Calling an American a seppo possibly conveys a more offhand and distant attitude than calling him a septic.

Forms Ending in -ie

aussie	Australian	bottie	bottle; bottom
barbie	barbecue	brekkie	breakfast
bickies	biscuits; dollars	brickie	bricklayer
bikie	motorbike rider	Brizzie	Brisbane
Blundies	Blundstone	cabbie	cabdriver
	workman boots	cardie	cardigan
boatie	person who sails	chalkie	school teacher
	boats	chappie	man
bookie	horse racing	chewie	chewing gum
	bookmaker	chippie	carpenter

chockie	chocolate
Chrissie	Christmas
ciggie	cigarette
commie	communist
conchie	conscientious person; conscientious objector
druggie	drug addict
flattie	flat-heeled shoe; flathead (fish); flat tyre
foodie	a gourmet
freebie	something for free
frenchie	condom
gladdie	gladiolus
goalie	goal-keeper
goodies	little treats
greenie	environmentalist
grommie	grommet (young surfer)
hollies	holidays
hottie	hotwater bottle
hungies	hungry
jarmies	pyjamas
kiddies	children
lammie	lamington
leckie	electric blanket
lippie	lipstick
littlies	little ones/ children
meanie	mean person
newie	new item
oldies	one's parents; old item
pollie	politician
pokies	poker machines
pozzie	position

HIZZIE?

According to *The Story of English* (Penguin Books, 1986), well-known Aussie performer Barry Humphries claimed he once heard an Australian woman describing her hospital visit for a hysterectomy as 'having a hizzie in the hozzie'.

postie	mail deliverer
premmie	prematurely born baby
prezzie	present
prozzie	prostitute
pull a	to put one over
swiftie	someone
quickie	anything done in a hurry; quick sex
rellies	one's relatives
rollie	'roll-your-own' cigarette
shrewdie	shrewd person
sickie	day off sick or supposedly sick
smoothie	smooth talker; drink made with blended fruit

GENERAL AUSSIE ENGLISH

sparkie	electrician	uni	university
subbie	sub-contractor	Vinnies	St Vincent de
sunnies	sunglasses		Paul's op shop
swiftie	trick		(an organisation
taddie	tadpole		like the Salvation
Tassie	Tasmania		Army)
	(pronounced 'tazzie')	weakie	a weak person
tinnie	can of beer	wharfie	a wharf labourer
townie	town person	Windies	the West Indian
trannie	transistor radio;		cricket team
	transvestite	Woolies	Woolworths (shop)
truckie	truckdriver	woollies	woollen clothing
U-ie	U-turn in a car	yachtie	a person who loves
umpie	the umpire		sailing yachts
undies	underwear	youngie	a young person

Forms Ending in -y

It's not unusual to find words ending in -ie also spelled with a -y ending. Thus a cabbie could well be a cabby. However some always take -ie and others always for some inscrutable reason take -y.

backy	tobacco	footy	football
Bundy	Bundaberg rum	kindy	kindergarten
comfy	comfortable	lavvy	lavatory
divvy van	police divisional van	placky	plastic
dunny	toilet	Rocky	Rockhampton
esky	portable ice-box	telly	TV
exxy	expensive		

Forms Ending in -o

There's the same kind of overlap between words ending in -ie or -y and words ending in -o. Some can be either, some are always one or the other. The following, however, always take -o:

avo	avocado	compo	compensation
ammo	ammunition	demo	demonstration
arvo	afternoon	dero	derelict person
combo	combination	doco	documentary film

evo	evening	rego	car registration
Freo	Fremantle	relo	relative
garbo	garbage collector	Salvo	Salvation Army
gyno	gynaecologist		member
info	information	servo	petrol station
intro	introduction	smoko	break for coffee, tea
journo	journalist		or a cigarette
kero	kerosene	speedo	speedometer
lezzo	lesbian	vego	vegetarian person or
metho	methylated spirits		meal (pronounced
milko	milkman		'vedjo')
muso	musician	wino	an alcoholic who
porno	pornography		drinks cheap wine

Personal Names

Australians are also keen to change people's names into diminutive forms, in the same way that they like to change all words into diminutives as shown above.

Most famous Australians are affectionately known by versions of their first names or surnames ending in the sound -ie (spelt in various ways). For example, the singer Jimmy Barnes is known as Barnsey. Oddly, some other names that already end in an -ie sound (like Kylie) are often transformed into something else again (perhaps Kyles). Some people's names are transformed with the ending -o; the most famous examples are the former sporting stars Jeff Thomson and Mark Jackson, known as Thommo and Jacko respectively.

Barry	Bazza	Murray	Muzza	Karen	Kazza
Kerry	Kezza	Garry	Gazza	Sharon	Shazza
John	Johnno	Terry	Tezza		

THEY MAY SAY ...

Aussies have a number of loving terms for 'toilet':

boghouse	lav/lavvy	thunderbox
crapper	loo	toilie
dunny	throne	toot ('oo' as in 'put')

MAD AS A CUT SNAKE

anger	mad as a cut snake	mad as a maggot
	mad as a meataxe	mad as a hornet
	mad as a frilled lizard	
insanity	off one's scone/rocker	silly as a wheel
	mad as a gumtree	silly as a bagful
	full of galahs	of worms
	mad as a mother-	a kangaroo loose in
	in-law's cat	the top paddock

MAD AS A CUT SNAKE

sadness	miserable as a shag on a rock happy as a bastard on Father's Day	miserable as a bandicoot
happiness	happy as a dog with two tails	happy as Larry (possibly after the Australian boxer Larry Foley, 1849-1917)
crudeness	rough as guts rough as a goat's knees	rough as bags rough as a pig's breakfast
weakness	weak as piss weak as water	weaker than a sun-burned snowflake
dryness	dry as a bone dry as a dead dingo's donger	dry as a nun's nasty dry as a chip dry as a pommy's towel
fullness	full as a goog full as a boot full to pussy's bow full as a tick	full as a footy final full as a bull's bum full as a state school hat-rack
invincibility	fit as a Mallee bull	game as Ned Kelly
uselessness	useful as a third armpit useful as a sore arse to a boundary rider	useful as a pocket on a singlet useful as a bucket under a bull

GENERAL AUSSIE ENGLISH

CHOOKS, CROCS & COCKIES

With a penchant for shortening words and creating phrases, it's not surprising that Aussies have given their friends (and foes) in the animal world a few 'special' names.

barra	barramundi
bitie	biting insect
blowie	blow fly
bluey	cattle dog
boomer	large kangaroo
brumby	wild horse
budgie	budgerigar
bug	small crab, as in Moreton Bay bug
bushman's clock	kookaburra
chook	chicken
cockie	cockatoo; cockroach
croc	crocodile
dunny budgie	fly
freshie	freshwater crocodile
joey	baby kangaroo
maggie	magpie
mozzie	mosquito
muddie	mud crab
neddie	horse
'roo	kangaroo
saltie	saltwater crocodile
sandie	sand crab
snapping log	crocodile
stinger	box jellyfish/sea wasp
woolly rocks	sheep
yabbie	small freshwater crayfish

GETTING AROUND WITH AUSSIE ENGLISH

These are the most striking cases of Australian words and Australian uses of general English words. Excluded are words and uses which are now familiar in all the main English-speaking countries, such as the originally American word 'truck', which is now usual in Australia too. Although most British people still call trucks 'lorries', they'll understand an American or an Australian who says 'trucks'.

Shopping & Eating

Akubra	famous brand of Aussie hat
bathers	swimsuit (Vic)
cozzie	swimsuit (NSW)
Driza-bone	famous brand of Aussie raincoat
haberdashery	a shop that sells sewing supplies, ribbons, etc
handbag	a woman's carry bag; a 'purse' in North America
hire purchase	what Americans call 'instalment buying'
jam	sweet fruit preserve; North Americans call it 'jelly'
jelly	gelatine dessert; 'jello' in North America
manchester	bed and bathroom linen
mince (meat)	called 'hamburger meat' in North America
moleskins	jeans made of brushed cotton
nappy	known as a 'diaper' by North Americans
petrol	called 'gas(oline)' in North America
pram	a 'baby buggy' in North America
purse	known as a 'change purse' in North America
spanner	a 'monkey wrench' in the USA
suspenders	straps worn to hold up stockings
thongs	rubber sandals/flip flops
threads	clothes
togs	swimsuit (Qld)

bumbag
  what Americans call a 'fanny pack'. Note that in Australia, 'fanny' is vulgar slang for female genitalia, so if you insist on using 'fanny pack' be prepared for either gasps or giggles.

GENERAL AUSSIE ENGLISH

chemist
: when it refers to a shop, this term roughly corresponds with the American drugstore or pharmacy (the latter term is also used in Australia) but the functions of a chemist are more restricted than those of an American drugstore

chips
: still often used to refer to (french) fries, as in the UK. Also used to refer to what the British call (potato) crisps.

daks
: men's trousers. Also used to describe tracksuit pants, as in trackie daks

entree
: on a restaurant menu this is a starter, not a main course as in some other countries

hamper
: large basket for food, especially used for picnics or presents, like a Christmas hamper

G'DAY, YA BASTARD!

In Australia, the word bastard has an extremely varied job description and it rarely (if ever) refers to illegitimacy. Used as a friendly, affectionate term – 'G'day, you old bastard!' – it can also be a handy term for a moment of compassion – 'Poor bastard lost his job'. But don't be fooled because an Aussie is just as likely to use bastard with a string of other abusive terms in a fiery exchange, or use it to describe something annoying, as in 'I can't fix this bastard of a thing!' or someone dispicable – 'He's a mean bastard'. To confuse you even more, this chameleon term is often used to describe *any* person, as in 'Should that bastard be fishing there?' Hint: either don't use this (bastard of a) term or just tread carefully during word experimentation.

lay-by
 reservation of an article by payment of a cash deposit, not a
 roadside stopping place as in the UK

prawn
 this can refer to a number of species of edible marine
 crustacean, some of them smaller than what American and
 British people would call a 'prawn' (shrimps etc)

skivvy
 long-sleeved, turtle-neck top made of stretch cotton and
 worn by either sex

stroller/pusher
 small wheeled trolley for shuttling around infants or small
 children, often called 'push chair' elsewhere

treacle
 what Australians call treacle is generally called 'molasses' by
 North Americans

vest
 a sleeveless outer garment, sometimes more formal with
 buttons like a waistcoat. It doesn't normally refer to a
 'singlet' as it does in the UK.

Land & Travel

caravan	what Americans call a '(house) trailer'
frontier	international boundary
median strip	dividing area between opposing traffic lanes
offsider	companion
park	means 'parking place', as in 'I'll try and find a park'
station	large stock farm, such as a cattle station

click
 kilometres, as in 'How many clicks to the next town?'

footpath
 a long narrow concrete strip used by pedestrians is usually
 called a footpath in Australia, whereas, when it's parallel
 with the road, it's called a 'sidewalk' in North America and a
 'pavement' in the UK

interstate
   'in/to another Australian state', as in 'Laura's gone interstate'
lane-way
   surfaced or unsurfaced passage, often between blocks
nature strip
   a vegetated strip by the side of the road, often between the
   road and the footpath. It's called a 'verge' in most other
   English-speaking countries.

HOUSEHOLD NAMES

POLITICIANS
Bob Hawke
   Labor Prime Minister 1983-91, former union leader,
   known also for his love of sport and colourful
   personal life

Paul Keating
   Labor Prime Minister 1991-96, famous for
   putting his hand on the Queen's back and being
   labelled the 'Lizard of Oz' by British tabloids

Jeff Kennett
   Liberal Premier of Victoria from 1992 who
   attracts strong feelings pro and con; famous for luring
   to Victoria a number of major national events and
   always seeking to add more; one of the few living
   people to have a verb based on his name, as in
   'We've been jeffed!'

Gough Whitlam
   Labor Prime Minister 1972-75, whose government
   was dismissed by the then Governor General, Sir
   John Kerr, in a questionable political manoeuvre.
   Since 1975 he's been an ambassador to UNESCO
   and head of the Australia-China Council.

paddock
> field, not necessarily one for grazing horses as in some other
> English-speaking countries

subway
> usually means 'pedestrian underpass', mainly at a train station;
> an underpass under a road is usually called an underpass!

ute
> small vehicle with a rectangular tray for transporting goods

Other Words & Verbs

bathroom	room with a bathtub, not necessarily with a toilet
burl	to try, as in 'Go on, give it a burl!'
cactus	of no further value; absolutely useless
cream	to defeat decisively
mongrel	horrible person
nought	zero, mainly used by older speakers
retrench	to make redundant, as in 'I got retrenched'

call
> when Australians use sentences like 'I'll call' they're nor-
> mally referring to making a telephone call, whereas in the
> UK 'to call' usually means 'to visit', as in 'I'll call in'

compulsory
> a change to the membership of a team can be described as
> 'compulsory' even if it's the result of an injury or illness
> rather than suspension

cooking with gas
> something going well and as planned

financial
> either 'in funds', as in 'I'm not feeling very financial today', or
> 'paid up', as in 'Only financial members of the club may vote'

fine up
> if the weather fines up, it means that the sun's come out

front up
> 'fronting up' is presenting oneself, making an appearance

problem
> sometimes refers to something which has already gone wrong and cannot be remedied, as in 'The delay to your letter was a problem for Australia Post'

randy
> libidinous; obviously not a popular choice by Australian parents for a child's name

rubbish
> pour scorn on, as in 'Jane was rubbishing the footy team'

queue
> 'standing in a queue', shared with British English, is 'standing in/on line'

smart
> well groomed, as in the UK, but the American sense of 'intelligent' is also very common

strife
> if you're 'in strife', you're in difficulties (not necessarily in an argument or fight)

surgery
> when used as an ordinary noun, as in 'I'm going to the surgery', this usually means 'doctor's office'

utilise
> put to use, used in more mundane situations than in other English-speaking countries

wash up
> refers to washing the dishes after a meal, whereas in North America this means washing the hands and face.

DID YOU KNOW ... The word cobber, an old-fashioned Aussie word for 'friend', stems from 'to cob' meaning 'to take a liking to someone', originally from a Suffolk dialect of the 1800s.

NATIONAL SONGS

The Australian National Anthem is 'Advance Australia Fair' which replaced the former anthem, 'God Save The Queen', in 1984. Most Australians grew up singing homage to the British Sovereign, and as a result sometimes struggle with the words of the newly adopted anthem. After an enthusiastic start in the first few bars, the words often fall into a musical mumble.

Waltzing Matilda

Another song that Australians know and love — and can sing with more gusto — is the unofficial national anthem, *Waltzing Matilda*. The words are as follows:

> *Once a jolly swagman camped by a billabong*
> *Under the shade of a coolibah tree,*

The swagman is a tramp or itinerant who carries his swag, his bundle of clothes, cooking implements, etc, tied up in a blanket or bedroll. The billabong is a waterhole, most often found in the bed of a river. The coolibah tree is a species of eucalypt found in inland Australia, often in areas which get flooded from time to time (hence the location near the billabong).

> *And he sang as he watched*
> *and waited till his billy boiled*
> *You'll come a-waltzing matilda with me.*

The billy is a tin container used for boiling water for tea. No-one is sure where the word comes from but it's probably from the Scottish 'bally', meaning bucket. The origin of the expression waltzing matilda is also uncertain but it probably dates back to a German influence on the goldfields. The German equivalent of a swag is Matilda, the 'girl' a man sleeps with when he's alone on the road. And the expression 'to waltz' is used in the context of German apprentices moving from one town to another to learn their trade. The Germans in this case would have come from the Barossa communities in South Australia. As a whole the phrase is the equivalent of being 'on the track', 'on the wallaby', 'on the road' (as a tramp).

> *Down came a jumbuck to drink at the billabong*
> *Up jumped the swagman and grabbed him with glee*
> *And he sang as he shoved that jumbuck in his tuckerbag*
> *You'll come a-waltzing matilda with me.*

The jumbuck is a sheep. This is thought to be Aboriginal pidgin for 'jump up', which is what the Aborigines presumably thought of as the most noticeable about sheep. The tuckerbag is the bag for food. Tucker is a British schoolboy word for food which still survives in Australian English.

> *Up rode the squatter mounted on his thoroughbred,*
> *Down came the troopers — one, two, three.*
> *Where's that jolly jumbuck you've got in your tuckerbag*
> *You'll come a-waltzing matilda with me.*

This is the strong arm of the law arriving to arrest the swagman for stealing the jumbuck. Squatters were originally people who pioneered settlement on land the government had not got around to allocating yet. They unofficially squatted on land that they were not legally supposed to have. Eventually of course the government came around to their point of view and they became wealthy landowners, part of the squattocracy, the new aristocracy of pastoral Australia. This squatter rides a thoroughbred horse and can summon troopers ('mounted police') to assist him.

> *But the swagman he up and he jumped in the waterhole,*
> *Drowning himself by the coolibah tree;*
> *And his ghost may be heard as it sings in the billabong*
> *You'll come a-waltzing matilda with me!*

REGIONAL DIFFERENCES

There are two schools of thought on this. One is anxious to suggest that different regional dialects are emerging in Australia. The other says that Australia is remarkable for its linguistic uniformity. Both schools are partly right. There's increasing evidence of regional differences, but compared to other English-speaking countries such differences are still not very numerous and not very major. This might seem surprising in terms of the large distances between Australian cities, but Australia was settled mainly along the coast in a rather short period and the mix of origins in the various cities was apparently fairly similar.

The most obvious differences involve vocabulary, and even those who stress the uniformity admit there are quite a few of these; but the regionalists claim difference not just in the words we use but in the way in which they are pronounced. It's claimed that a Melburnian can be distinguished from a Sydneysider, that

STATE OF EXCITEMENT

Each Australian State and Territory has a special name highlighting a feature of each place. You'll mainly see the following on some tourist posters and car number plates.

Apple Isle	Tasmania
Capital Territory	Australian Capital Territory
Festival State	South Australia
Garden State	Victoria
NT Outback Australia	Northern Territory
Premier State	New South Wales
State of Excitement	Western Australia
Sunshine State	Queensland

everyone can tell a Queenslander, and that the South Australians can be picked as soon as they say 'school'. As mentioned earlier, there are indeed differences in pronunciation but like most of the vocabulary differences these mainly involve tendencies rather than absolute contrasts. The differences are nowhere near as major as those which separate an Australian from a New Zealander who simply has to ask for 'fush and chups' to be identified and whose English is travelling further along its own track with each generation.

Most of the vocabulary differences aren't enough to cause much misunderstanding. The way Australians move around the country a lot has meant that it's increasingly difficult to pin these down to one particular area. The regions in this case are based more on patterns of settlement from colonial days than on state boundaries, and even now don't always coincide with the boundaries.

In many cases, when there's a difference, there'll be a general word used by all Australians and then the particular regional word. In some cases, however, there's no standard word, only the various regional words.

Some Australians would like to be different. They pick over the items of regional variation with delighted fascination, sounding as if they can barely wait until the dialect of Adelaide is as remote from the dialect of Sydney as Scottish English is from that of Yorkshire.

Most linguistic accounts of the regions of Australia are really accounts of the big cities, all of which, with the exception of the rather contrived city of Canberra, cling to the coastline. But, as already noted, there are also city-country differences within each state. There are many words and expressions which are region specific. Some of them are listed here and others can be found listed in other sections, particularly 'Borrowed Words' and 'Food & Drink'.

Here are some of the main concepts for which some of the states differ. It should be noted that the pattern of usage is more complex than this table suggests, and that visitors may encounter other words not listed in this table.

REGIONAL DIFFERENCES

While there may be many Perth dwellers who have never called a swimming costume 'bathers' and many Brisbanians that never call them 'togs', here's a list of terms generally typical of the different states.

NSW	QLD	SA	TAS	VIC	WA
costume worn when swimming					
cozzie	togs	bathers	bathers	bathers	bathers
10 oz glass of beer ~~pot~~					
middy	~~middy~~	schooner	pot	pot	pot
round slice of potato covered in batter and deep fried					
potato scallop	potato scallop	potato scallop	potato cake	potato cake	potato cake
fizzy drink with a dollop of ice-cream					
ice cream soda	ice cream soda *spider*	spider	spider	spider	ice cream soda
small red sausages at cocktail parties					
cocktail frankfurts	cheerios	frankfurts	saveloys; little boys	cocktail sausages	frankfurts
children's playground apparatus used for sliding down					
slippery dip/slide	slippery dip/slide	slippery dip/slide	slide	slide	slippery dip
smooth sandwich paste made from ground roasted peanuts					
peanut butter	peanut paste	peanut butter	peanut butter	peanut butter	peanut butter
non-alcoholic aerated sweet drink					
soft drink	cordial *soft drink*	soft drink	cordial	soft drink	soft drink
a common black and white bird					
magpie; peewee	magpie; peewee	Murray magpie; peewee	magpie; mudlark	magpie; mudlark	magpie
thin loop of rubber used for holding together small objects					
rubber band	rubber band	lacky band	rubber band	lacker band	rubber band
mid morning break at primary school					
playlunch; recess	little lunch	recess	playtime	playlunch	recess

VICTORIA

the Cabbage Garden

Victoria was once known as the cabbage-garden because of the State's early ability to produce fruit and vegetables from its rich soil and accommodating climate. Victorians there fore were referred to as Cabbage Gardeners, the implication being that that's probably all they're good for.

Mexicans

Another way of looking at Victorians has been to describe them as Mexicans, because from the point of view of New South Wales they are south of the border.

Melbourne

Melbourne was named in 1837 by Governor Bourke after Lord Melbourne, then British Prime Minister. Melbourne is more English in its appearance and inclinations than any other capital city. Its residents claim to live stylishly – to dine well and to dress well, to be as sophisticated as Sydney is flamboyant.

Melbourne is famous for its green and yellow trams. They provide a pleasant way to move around the city, although it can be a slow ride to the suburbs (the tram system was devised before speed meant everything). Watch out for the burgundy-coloured City Circle tram – a free service that loops the city centre. It used to be important to be polite to the connie, the tram conductor, but they no longer exist, much to everyone's disappointment.

Victorian Lingo

busy as Bourke Street

very busy, usually referring to traffic

the City Loop

the collective name for the four underground train stations in the city

hook turn

a driving manoeuvre which terrifies the rest of Australia in which to turn right at an intersection a motorist pulls over to the left of the road with the right-hand indicator flashing, and then crosses all lanes of traffic to complete the turn; made necessary by the fact that the trams occupy the middle ground

more front than Myer

used to describe a person who is very cheeky, not at all shy. Myer is a department store that originated in Melbourne.

the Paris end of Collins Street

the tree-lined length of Collins Street between Swanston and Spring Streets; at night the trees are lit by fairy lights

the Tan

a very popular 4km jogging track around Kings Domain and the Royal Botanical Gardens

Yarra banker

a soapbox orator on the banks of the Yarra River

BLACK TIE & A BEER CAN HAT

The Melbourne Cup

The country's biggest horse race still brings the nation to an almost eerie halt on the first Tuesday of each November, at 3.20 pm. The combination of betting and stopping work for the two mile (3.2km) event proves to be irresistible. Held at the Flemington race track in the city's inner west since 1861, the event is a curious mix of elegantly turned out society types and the boisterous masses enjoying the chance to dress up in black tie while wearing a hat topped with beer cans. The rest of the country joins Cup Sweeps, choosing horses by chance, or actually placing a bet for possibly the only time of the year. It's rare to find an Aussie, especially a Melburnian, who isn't having some sort of flutter (bet) on the horses on this day.

NEW SOUTH WALES

Cornstalks

New South Welshmen have sometimes been called cornstalks. It seems that quite early in colonial days the climate and way of life agreed with the newcomers so that the men who grew up in Australia became noted for their height and slim build. They grew like cornstalks, with the characteristic body tapering from broad shoulders to slim hips.

ROSELLA JAM

A woman moved from Queensland, where 'rosellas' are a type of fruit, to Northern NSW where they're birds. She asked a local if he could get her some rosellas. After asking her if two would suffice, he was understandably sur- prised when she said she'd need more as she wanted to make jam!

Sydney

Sydneysiders believe that Sydney is 'where it's at' and that's all there is to say, a point of view which irritates the Melburnians in particular. But with the Bridge and the Opera House and one of the finest harbours in the world, and a generally hedonistic climate, they don't care what the Melburnians say. Sydney was named by Governor Arthur Phillip (1738-1814) the British naval officer who brought the First Fleet to Sydney Cove, in honour of Thomas Townshend, 1st Viscount Sydney, who was Secretary of the Home Department at the time.

up a gum tree

Apart from naming Sydney, Governor Arthur Phillip is the first person to have recorded the term 'gum tree' for a eucalypt in his journal of 1789. The name was considered apt because the substance oozing from the tree was thought to be a kind of gum. Fifty years later it's clear that the colony had not only identified gum trees but knew what it's like to be up them.

This usage follows the American phrase 'up a tree' which refers to an animal being trapped in a tree. In the Australian context 'up a gum tree' came to mean 'in a state of confusion' or 'in a hopeless predicament'. The first recorded example of the phrase in use was a settler commenting on the behaviour of his workforce: 'My convicts were always drinking rum, I often wished they were up a gumtree'. Employer/employee relationships in Australia have struggled to rise from this low point.

NSW Expressions

shoot through like a Bondi tram

Some places are cultural icons: Bondi Beach is one of them. Australians have an image of this particular beach watched over by a kind of beach version of the Aussie digger, the Aussie lifesaver. At one stage, when Sydney had trams, there was a tram that went to Bondi. Apparently there was a stretch of the track near Centennial Park when the tram picked up speed and went noticeably fast. Nowadays,

to shoot through like a Bondi tram is basically to leave very quickly or bugger off.

up the Cross
If Bondi Beach is everything that's fine in life, then King's Cross is everything that's sinful. These days it's a little out classed by Oxford Street, home of the annual Gay Mardi Gras, but to go up the Cross is still to enter a bohemian world.

the Coathanger
this is an irreverent name for the Harbour Bridge

Pitt Street farmer
a city businessman who channels money into country property – wears a suit during the week; moleskins and workman boots on the weekends

SOUTH AUSTRALIA
Known as the Festival State, it could well have been named the Empty State with only 1% of its population inhabiting a whopping 80% of the state's land. As well as being home to some of Australia's leading wine districts, South Australia can also claim fame as the only Australian colony never to have admitted convicts.

Croweaters
South Australians have been known as Croweaters. The story behind this nickname is that life was so hard in South Australia that the colonials would very likely run short of sheep for the dinner table and be forced to eat crows.

Adelaide
Adelaide is a pleasant town, well-heeled and respectable, as easy to live in as a country town and as interesting as an international city. It's named after Queen Adelaide, the wife of William IV. Its biggest claim to being acknowledged as a city with big ideas is the Adelaide Arts Festival, a biennial affair which draws local and international talent.

South Australian Lingo

fritz
>also known as 'bung fritz'. This is the SA equivalent of devon. There's a strong German community near Adelaide.

donkey
>to give someone a ride on the back of your bike – what other Australians would refer to as either a dink or a dinky

Stobie pole
>the telegraph pole made of concrete and steel named after the creator, JC Stobie

WESTERN AUSTRALIA

Western Australia is the largest state, encompassing extremes of terrain and climate. As a result words like 'remote' and 'isolated' are likely to turn up, as in terms like isolated child, isolated class, isolated school, isolated pharmacy, or remote posting, remote resident, remote site.

Sandgropers
>Western Australians are called Sandgropers because most of the state is desert. To sandgrope is to walk in soft sand, a procedure that most people find tiring. Sandgroper is shortened to Groper. The Gropers of course live in Groperland.

Westralia
>Western Australia is sometimes referred to as Westralia, so Western Australians are Westralians.

QUOKKA

Alarmed by the number of what appeared to be huge 'rats' on the sandy island 19 kms off the WA coast, the Dutch explorer De Vlamingh named the island in their honour – 'Rottnest', literally, 'Rat's Nest'. In fact, the curious creatures weren't 'rats' at all, but the Australian native quokka.

Perth

Perth is separated from the rest of Australia by the Nullarbor Plain (Nullarbor being Latin 'nulla arbor' meaning 'no tree') – it's claimed to be the most isolated capital city in the world. Perth was named by Captain James Stirling after the city of the same name in Scotland.

On the whole, people in Perth show no sign of missing the rest of Australia, being entirely content with the beautiful city they have and rather inclined to think on the contrary that they would be better off without the rest of the country. Indeed West Australians refer to East Coast inhabitants as t'othersiders and Eastern Staters, and this is usually in tones of disparagement.

RED INFESTATION

Off the coast of WA is an Australian protectorate, Christmas Island. It's famous for the summer infestation of red crabs that migrate from the rainforest to the coast.

Locals have such irksome stories as finding these critters in their footy boots and under their pillows!

Western Australian Lingo

the doctor
  the cool sea breeze which blows inland in the late afternoon and is identified variously depending on where you are. In Perth it's known as the Fremantle doctor because it blows into Perth from the direction of Fremantle.

Nyungar
  a West Australian Aborigine. In a local Aboriginal language nyungar means 'man'.

skimpy
  a scantily clad barmaid

'Kal' & 'Rotto'
  these are what the locals call Kalgoorlie and Rottnest Island

NORTHERN TERRITORY

Top Enders

The inhabitants of the Northern Territory are known as Territorians, naturally enough, or as Top Enders, again naturally enough. A top end would presuppose a bottom end but this doesn't seem to happen. The only other place where the top end/bottom end distinction applies seems to be the Murray River where the bottom end is towards the mouth and the dividing line between top and bottom is marked by the conjunction of the Murray and Darling Rivers.

Darwin

Darwin was named after Charles Darwin, the English naturalist, who visited Australia aboard HMS Beagle in 1836. Darwin has always been the most multicultural of Australian cities. There's always been constant traffic between the neighbouring Asian islands to the north and the Top End of Australia. The result of this, for example, is the extraordinary Asian food markets particularly on Mindil Beach, and the fact that Darwin folk were eating laksa for years before it ever appeared on the menus of Sydney and Melbourne.

Northern Territory Lingo

the Wet

the monsoon season

the Dry

the opposite of the Wet; the final stage of this is referred to as the build-up and causes great irritability among the inhabitants

Darwin rig or Territory rig

a style of casual dress for men that's suitable for the humid weather conditions of the Northern Territory; usually a short-sleeved, open neck shirt and trousers. Territory formal means a long-sleeved shirt and tie – no jacket required. You'll either hear these terms mentioned verbally or written at the bottom of invitations.

QUEENSLAND

Known as the Sunshine State, Queensland certainly has its fair share of sunshine and places in which to enjoy it. The coast is amiable but inland Queensland stretching up towards Cape York is as tough a strip of the outback as anyone will ever encounter. Towards the North is a region called the Channel Country in which numerous interlocking rivers regularly flood to form an inland sea.

Bananaland
> Queensland is known as Bananaland and its inhabitants as Bananabenders, because of the big banana plantations on its south-eastern coast

Brisbane

Brisbane was established as a convict settlement for the worst kind of offenders. It was named after Sir Thomas Brisbane, who was governor of NSW from 1821 to 1825. It's celebrated in song as a place of ultimate despair. Notwithstanding this grim past, it's emerged as a rather hedonistic city which can be a bit steamy in summer but which to compensate has the most beautiful clear, sunny winter.

Queensland Lingo

duchess
> dressing table

the Ekka
> the Royal Brisbane Exhibition held at the exhibition grounds in mid-August

the Gabba
> the Brisbane Cricket Ground, so called because of its location in the suburb of Woollongabba

port
> a suitcase – short for 'portmanteau'

schoolies' week
>   the rowdy end-of year festivities for high school graduates
>   after their final exams, usually centred around the Gold
>   Coast

windsor sausage
>   type of processed meat – sold as devon, fritz and polony in
>   other States

TASMANIA

Tasmanians feel they are often overlooked by the rest of Australia which they refer to as the Mainland, the inhabitants being Mainlanders. And certainly something seems to get lost in the translation over Bass Strait, so that Tasmania and the rest of Australia are never quite on the same wave-length. Tasmania has some of the most beautiful scenery in the world and parts of it are still quite wild and inaccessible. The South Coast in particular, where the Roaring Forties fetch up, is remote, dangerous and beautiful.

Apple Isle
>   this name refers to Tasmania's past success in growing
>   apples, although current crops don't feature the apple in
>   quite the same way; the inhabitants are sometimes referred
>   to as Apple Islanders

Tassie
>   an affectionate shortening of the name Tasmania is also a
>   common name for a Tasmanian; Taswegian is another
>   variation but not as common

Hobart

Hobart is the second oldest city in Australia – the first convict settlement being at Sydney Cove and the second being established in Hobart in 1804. The city has an old-world charm – a fishing village character marked by Georgian houses and docks, with Mount Wellington towering above it. Hobart was named after Robert Hobart, fourth Earl of Buckinghamshire and Secretary of State for War and the Colonies (1801-04). A rivalry exists between Hobart and Launceston which is similar to the tension between Sydney and Melbourne. So whatever Hobart gets, Launceston has to equal or do better.

Tasmanian Lingo

mutton bird
> a species of shearwater which nests on islands off Tasmania and which is considered a gourmet item; it's extremely oily

chalet
> an outhouse or small dwelling in the garden of a main dwelling

Many rural Tasmanians refer to trees as if they're male ('We felled him last week').

RIDE THE WILD PENNY!

Penny Farthing Championships
Evandale, Tasmania, is the home of this sporting event with a difference. Thousands from Dusseldorf to Dubbo swarm to this ye olde Tassie village to experience the world's largest gathering of Penny Farthing competitors and admirers. Sporting events include the Obstacle Race, the 200m Sprint and the Slow Ride which awards blue ribbon status to the rider who finishes last! (It takes amazing skill to steer a Penny Farthing to victory at a snail's pace.) Evandale hosts these sporting championships – and a lively village fair – each year on the last weekend of February.

THE AUSTRALIAN CAPITAL TERRITORY

The Australian Government Territory is the small area of land surrounding Canberra, the metropolis that is the capital city of Australia. As befits a government creation it hasn't really got any nicknames; abuse yes, nicknames no!

Canberra

Canberra has the feel of a plush country town, the country town of some people's wildest dreams. It's a unique blend of town, gown and public service with politicians who zap in for the season in Parliament, and zap out again as fast as their planes can carry them.

> ### SHOCKWAVES
>
> If you're interested in hearing the goings on in Australian Parliament when it's in session, tune in to *ABC News Radio*, broadcast nationally on the AM band.

The name 'Canberra' is an anglicisation of the Aboriginal name of the area. Walter Burley Griffin (1876-1937) an Australian architect born in the USA, created the original design of Canberra. People are still divided about the concept. Almost everyone agrees that they immediately get lost in Canberra, and some abuse has been hurled at Griffin by those who spend weary hours attempting to escape the endless loops and whirls that are Canberra's streetscape.

Canberra Lingo

bush week
  the name of end-of-term student celebrations at the Australian National University

govie/guvvie home
  a government-funded residence usually offering low rent; an ex-govie is one of these residences being offered on the open market

govie/guvvie school
  a government-funded school ('state school' elsewhere)

OTHER REGIONS

There are a few other areas of Australia which emerge from the map as having a distinct identity.

The Riverina (& Sunraysia)

The lifeline of the Riverina is the Murray River, which feeds off the waters from the Snowy Mountains and then flows all the way to St Vincent's Gulf in South Australia. The area known as Sunraysia is centred on Mildura and has sprung up around an

HOUSEHOLD NAMES

MEDIA ENTERTAINERS

Ita Buttrose
   prominent in the publishing industry for over 20 years, she has also made valuable contributions to AIDS research and awareness as well as other causes. She was awarded an OBE in1979 and an Order of Australia medal in 1988.

Ian 'Molly' Meldrum
   known for his contributions to the Australian music industry; keeps Australians informed about the world pop music scene

Bert Newton
   very popular and cheesy TV host – one of the originals of Australian television – who currently hosts an morning programme, appearing on TV for a world record-breaking 2.5 hours a day, five days a week, all year. Nicknamed 'Moonface'.

Ray Martin
   TV current affairs presenter and winner of several popularity awards

Maggie Tabberer
   fashion icon who is now also involved in community work; recently awarded an Order of Australia

irrigation scheme developed in 1923, which has made the dried fruit industry and vineyards of the region possible.

New England

New England, northeast of Sydney, is the district which claims the university town of Armidale as its centre. It's a farming and mining district – the name 'New England' has to be seen as wishful thinking on the part of the settlers.

HOUSEHOLD NAMES

ACTORS & ENTERTAINERS

Paul Hogan
comic actor, previously Sydney Harbour Bridge painter and then TV comedian; known for the *Crocodile Dundee* movies and for his ads enticing Americans to visit Australia, including the immortal invitation to 'throw another shrimp on the barbie'

Barry Humphries
comedian who portrays various quintessentially Australian characters including Dame Edna Everidge and Sir Les Patterson

Nicole Kidman
hugely successful Hollywood actor, married to Tom Cruise

Kylie Minogue   singer and actor

Elle Macpherson
long-legged international supermodel; she's sometimes referred to as 'The Body'

Olivia Newton-John
singer and actor, best known for her role in the 1978 film *Grease*

Skippy
kangaroo in a much-loved children's TV series

REGIONAL DIFFERENCES

BRICKIE'S CLEAVAGE

A brickie's cleavage is the exposed top of the buttocks peeping over the rim of a pair of shorts. Here are a few more eye-catching body-part terms you may encounter.

beak	nose	face fungus	beard; facial hair
block	head	gregory peck	neck
bum	buttocks	honker	nose
bunghole	mouth	ivories	teeth
breadbasket	stomach	laughing gear	mouth
cakehole	mouth	loaf/scone	head
clodhoppers	feet	lugs	ears
crockery	teeth	noggin	head or brains
dial	face	plates of meat	feet

The Alice

This is the local name for Alice Springs, a town in central Australia in the southern part of the Northern Territory. Relatively close by is Uluru (formerly called Ayers Rock). Alice Springs was named after Alice Todd, the wife of Charles Todd who was responsible for the construction of the Overland Telegraph Line which connected Darwin to Adelaide and which was completed in 1872.

The Gold Coast

The strip of coastline just south of Brisbane is known as the Gold Coast. It's a tourist phenomenon – high-rise perched on the edge of the beach. It's been so successful that it's now rivalled by other 'coasts' – the Sunshine Coast (further north than the Gold Coast in Queensland) and the Capricorn Coast (the coastline near Rockhampton). New South Wales is divided into the South Coast (the Shoalhaven River to the Victorian border), the Central Coast (from the Hawkesbury River to Lake Macquarie) and the North Coast (from the Manning River to the Queensland border).

BORROWED WORDS

US INFLUENCE

As already mentioned, the basic British influence in Australian English has been overlaid since WWII by a strong US presence, largely felt in the media. It's an indication of the speed at which American words can now move into Australian that it took only six months for 'couch potato' to travel from the pages of a New York magazine (mid-1987) to a Melbourne newspaper (December 1987). Australians don't borrow everything that's new in American English – they take their pick. Among the popular US items which made it into Australian English in the 1980s and 1990s are:

bag lady
　　an elderly woman who's homeless and who carries all her
　　belongings in a shopping bag
cockamamie
　　crazy; ridiculous; all muddled up
cornball
　　sentimentalist who is given to trite and hackneyed sayings
cyberspace
　　the world inhabited by intrepid travellers on the Internet
　　which is made to seem like another world; but which at its
　　most fundamental is simply the network of all the comput-
　　ers that are linked up to each other via the telephone lines
deep throat
　　anonymous informant within an organisation who leaks
　　information to an outsider
d'oh
　　this now ubiquitous expression made famous by Homer
　　Simpson is meant to indicate that you're reprimanding
　　yourself for some new piece of stupidity
dork
　　fool, particularly someone who's socially clumsy, dresses
　　badly, and generally makes an idiot of himself; also called

(but less commonly in Australia) a 'dweeb'; both these words are attempting to replace the Australian expression dag

life in the fast lane
this is 80s talk – at the height of 'yuppiedom' life in the fast lane was 'where it was at'

fast track
move something along in a process at unusual and irregular speed

mover and shaker
important and influential person who makes things happen

parlay
convert a sum of money into an even larger sum by taking a gamble with it

psychobabble
the jargon of psychology, particularly that relates to psychotherapy groups

spin control
the kind of slant that can be given to anything that happens by the people who run the media campaign for a politician

a tad
a little; there's a theory that it's a shortening of 'tadpole' as applied to a small child (also used in parts of England)

underclass
the people who are never caught up by society's safety nets and who form a class of their own with a lifestyle, culture and set of values entirely at odds with mainstream society

wimp
weak, effeminate, cowardly person; this word is being overtaken by wuss or wussy but is still popular

---

THEY MAY SAY ...

Clobber, a term for clothes, can be traced back to the phrase 'clubbered up' meaning 'dressed up'.
Originating in Kent, the word has a Romany history.

UK INFLUENCE

Australian English hasn't lost touch with the UK entirely, however. A few items of British English are also still going strong.

aggro
> aggressive, as in 'Don't be so aggro'; the Australian use is slightly different from the British one – Australians don't really talk about 'giving people aggro'

bonk
> a half-joking, half-euphemistic word for having sex

gobsmacked
> astonished. The image that lurks behind this word is the reflex action of the hand cover the gaping mouth ('gob') after an enormous shock.

naff off
> Princess Anne told some journalists to 'naff off' once and has never been allowed to forget it

minder
> the television program *Minder* was very popular, so a few expressions have drifted through from it, but the word 'minder' no longer applies to a 'crook's' bodyguard, but to anyone whose job it is to shield someone else from all kinds of unpleasantness (pop stars have minders, as do politicians)

BILLY BALLY

Billy may sound purely Australian, but the word hails back to the Scottish word 'bally' meaning 'milk pail'. Aussie phrases using billy include the rhyming slang billy lids for 'kids' and billy tea.

Mixed USA/UK Influence

With regard to vocabulary, it's interesting that Australia has categorically, but inconsistently, selected particular British and American terms as its first choice of reference. For example, Australian 'truck' drivers (American) or truckies rather than 'lorry' drivers (British) visit 'petrol' stations (British) rather than 'gas' stations (American).

ABORIGINAL INFLUENCE

There isn't a huge number of words in Australian English that are borrowed from Aboriginal languages – in fact, about 440 – but they flavour the language in that they're significant cultural items. The pattern of borrowing is fairly straightforward and follows the pattern of European settlement in Australia. Captain Cook set the precedent with kangaroo. To European eyes this was an extraordinary animal and quite unlike anything they'd ever come across. So while there were many plants and animals that could be named a native this or that – the koala was originally called a 'native bear' and the angophora was called the 'native apple' – this creature couldn't be thought of as a native anything. So Captain Cook asked the Aborigines of the Guugu Yimidhirr tribe of North Queensland what they called it, he noted kangaroo in his diary, and thus the first major borrowing into Australian English came about.

There's a curious sequel to this story. Relations between Aborigines and Europeans in Australia went from bad to worse, so that after that first great influx of Aboriginal words in the colonial period of Australian history there was then no traffic between Aboriginal languages and Australian English. What was worse was that there was little record of Aboriginal languages kept, so that when people finally became interested enough to attempt to track down the origin of kangaroo, they couldn't find the word for kangaroo in the local language. They were possibly thrown off by the fact that whereas in English the difference between the 'k' consonant and the 'g' consonant is significant, in the language of the Guugu Yimidhirr there was seen to be no difference at all. While this was being sorted out, the folklore theory developed that in fact Cook had been hoodwinked by the Aborigines and that the word kangaroo meant 'I don't know'. Alternatively it meant something very rude. The misunderstanding has been sorted out – kangaroo means 'kangaroo' in anyone's language, but the folklore still persists.

Borrowings into Australian English have been made from a number of different Aboriginal languages, depending on where the Europeans turned up, the largest number of borrowings being from languages of the eastern coast. They're mostly names of animals and plants.

• The Sydney Region

bogie	swimming hole
bombora	current over a submerged reef
boobook	a small owl or mopoke
boomerang	curved piece of wood used as a missile
bettong	rat-kangaroo
corella	large parrot, predominantly white with pink or orange-red markings
corroboree	Aboriginal ceremony
currawong	large black and white bird with yellow eyes and a loud ringing call
dingo	native dog
geebung	small tree
gibber	rock or stone
gin	Aboriginal woman
gunyah	rough shelter or dwelling
koala	'bear-like' marsupial
kurrajong	tree
myall	wild, from an Aboriginal word meaning 'stranger'
nulla-nulla	Aboriginal club or weapon
pademelon	wallaby
potoroo	small wallaby
wallaby	small kangaroo
waratah	flower with large showy red flowers, the emblem of New South Wales
warrigal	dingo
wombat	marsupial the size of a small pig which lives in a burrow and is nocturnal
woomera	Aboriginal weapon

BORROWED WORDS

BORROWED WORDS

- ### Southern Victoria

bingie	stomach or belly	luderick	fish
belah	tree	yabba	talk

- ### Tasmania

lubra	Aboriginal woman

- ### Southern South Australia

joey	kangaroo young	wurley	rough shelter
willy-willy	sudden circling gust of wind		

- ### The Perth Region

bardy	edible grub	marron	crayfish
euro	wallaby	quokka	small wallaby
jarrah	large eucalypt	wandoo	eucalypt
karri	eucalypt	wongi	talk (verb)
kylie	boomerang		

- ### Inland Victoria

mallee	tree	mulga	type of wattle
mia-mia	rough shelter		

- ### Inland New South Wales

billabong	waterhole	coolamon	wooden dish
brigalow	tree	gidgee	tree
brolga	bird	quandong	tree with edible fruit
budgerigar	small, brightly coloured bird	yarraman	horse

> **DID YOU KNOW ...** Mulga Bill is a fictional character in the poem by AB 'Banjo' Paterson, *Mulga Bill's Bicycle*, written in 1896.

- **The Brisbane Region**

barramundi	fish
dilly	bag made of twisted grass or fibre
yakka	work

- **North Queensland**

cooee	cry made to signal one's presence in the bush
kangaroo	kangaroo

- **The Outback**

coolabah	tree
nardoo	fern

HARD YAKKA

Yakka is a popular brand of work clothes used by labourers, electricians (sparkies), carpenters (woodies), plumbers and others who work in the construction industry. They're also popular with university students who have 'lefty' tendencies.

It's obligatory to complete this outfit with a pair of blundies – Blundstone boots.

Recent Times

In the last 10 years or so there's been another shifting in the status of Aboriginal languages and of Australian English, with the result that after decades of no borrowings at all there are now some new additions. A notable one is Koori, a word from the Awakabal tribe near Newcastle, just north of Sydney. Koori has been used by some Aborigines to refer to an Aborigine of eastern Australia since the early part of this century.

This shift in attitude is also noticeable in place names, beginning with the reinstating of the Loritdja word for that great red monolith in Central Australia, Uluru, formerly known as Ayers Rock. Similarly the Olgas are now the Kata Tjuta, as they've been known for a very long while apart from the small period of European settlement.

BORROWED WORDS

The following are some placenames that have been anglicised along with their meaning:

Allora	'waterhole'; a town in Queensland
Amaroo	'beautiful place' or 'red mud' or 'rain'; a town in NSW
Babinda	'waterfall'; a town in Queensland
Dandenong	'lofty mountain', a mountain range in Victoria
Dorrigo	'stringybark'; a town in NSW
Dunedoo	'swan'; a town in NSW
Ekibin	a part of the river where Aborigines obtained edible aquatic roots; a locality in Brisbane
Murrumbidgee	'big water'; a river in NSW
Narooma	'blue water'; a town in NSW
Wagga Wagga	'crows'; a town in NSW
Waikerie	'wings or anything that flies'; a town in South Australia
Ulladulla	'safe harbour'; a coastal town in NSW

Sometimes these anglicised names and meanings originate from Aboriginal legends; legends which have been taken aboard by English speakers:

Arkaroola

town in the northern Flinders Range in South Australia. The place of Arkaroo is named after a great legendary Dreamtime snake which drank Lake Frome dry and carved out the bed of the Arkoola Creek which then filled by passing water.

Gidgealpaa

town in South Australia. The meaning is 'to stand in the shade of a grey rain cloud', a reference to Kilyalpani, one of the mythical women who created the land. She once prayed for rain and while she was praying a grey cloud formed above her.

Aboriginal Myths

Whatever the successes and failures of Aboriginal words in Australian English, a small set of them are entrenched in the national folklore. What would Australia be without the bunyip, that mythical creature who lives in the waterhole and is thought to cause loud noises at night and to devour women and children. The bunyip comes to us from Wemba-Wemba, a language of western Victoria, and was first reported in the Port Philip Herald in 1847. An interesting description appears in the same year in Bell's Life in Sydney 19 June. 'That apochryphal animal of many names, commonly designated The Bunyip has, accord-

---

HOUSEHOLD NAMES

SPORTING STARS

Michael Doohan
multiple world 500cc motorcycle champion

Dawn Fraser
former champion Olympic swimmer and now tireless community worker; recently awarded an Order of Australia

Cathy Freeman
outstandingly successful Aboriginal middle-distance runner

Andrew Gaze
basketball star

Greg Norman
world-class golfer, winner of several majors and known as the 'Great White Shark'

Kieran Perkins
great long-distance Olympic swimmer who holds world records

ing to a correspondent of the Sydney Morning Herald, been seen on the Murrumbidgee. It's described as being about as big as a six months old calf, of dark brown colour, a long neck, a long pointed head, large ears, a thick mane of hair from the head down the neck, and two large tusks. It's said to be an amphibious animal, as it has been observed floundering in the rivers, as well as grazing on their banks.'

The mindi, from Wemba-Wemba, is a mythical hairy snake which also lies in wait at waterholes. Mythologically speaking, waterholes seem to be extremely dangerous places. You should watch out for the yowie which comes from the Yuwaalaraay of northern New South Wales. The yowie is a huge ape-like monster, a kind of Australian bigfoot – the Aboriginal word translates as 'dream spirit'. And finally, you should beware of the min-min light, a will-o'-the-wisp which is regarded as an evil apparition and which turns up on the plains of northern Queensland.

DRONGO, LIAR, RATBAG

Politics

Short of actually calling each other liars, Australian politicians positively pride in inventing colourful names for each other. Drongo, dingbat, ratbag, sheep, scum, idiot, great galah and silly old bugger are some of the terms let fly from the parliamentary benches. Former prime minister Paul Keating was an acknowledged master; once asked if one-time rival Andrew Peacock would make a comeback, he said 'a souffle doesn't rise twice'. When the ABC began broadcasting into Asia, it found that *Parliamentry Question Time* was one of the most popular shows; viewers from Singapore to the Philippines apparently got a kick out of the entertaining abuse.

DIFFERENCES

Despite the shared origin of Australian English and other Englishes there are quite a few differences. Here are some of the most common examples:

American English

Australian English	*American English*
barrack for	root for
bonnet	car hood
boot	trunk
braces (holds up trousers)	suspenders
camp bed; stretcher	cot
capsicum	(bell) peppers
cot	crib
cyclone	hurricane
dry biscuits	crackers
fringe (hair)	bangs
ground floor	first floor
lollies	candy
takeaway	takeout
uni	college

British English

Australian English	*British English*
bank teller	(bank) cashier
bushwalking	walking/hiking
eggplant	aubergine
freeway	motorway
garbo	dustman
highway	dual carriageway
icy-pole/ice-block	(ice) lolly
lollies	sweets
overseas	abroad
paddock	field
private school	public school

public holiday	bank holiday
wharfie	docker
windsheater	sweatshirt
zucchini	courgette

New Zealand English

Australian English	New Zealand English
abattoir/slaughterhouse	freezing works
bitumen road	tarseal road
bloke	joker (also heard in Australia, though less frequently)
doona	duvet (also used in the UK)
esky (portable ice box)	coolie bin
gravel/dirt road	metal road
holiday home	bach/crib (mainly Otago)
milkbar; grocery store; deli	dairy (also heard in parts of Australia)
plot; small block of land	section (also heard in Australia)
speed humps/bumps	judder bars
thongs/sandals	jandals
bushwalking	tramping
uni	varsity (also still heard in the UK but mainly for Oxford and Cambridge)

Of course New Zealand English also has a considerable number of Maori loan words, corresponding with words from Aboriginal languages in Australian English.

The traditional, Anglo-inspired dinner of 'meat and three veg' followed by stewed fruit (out of a tin) and custard or jelly (out of a packet) has in the last 10 to 20 years been ousted by a culinary amalgam of all that Australia's multicultural society and multifarious landscapes have to offer. The new 'Australian style' is still emerging and it takes in the full range of ethnically authentic migrant cuisines as well as the boldly innovative style of Australia's best restaurateurs and chefs. What it means for the visitor, at least in the major cities, is a vast choice in good-value and interesting eating.

Not so long ago Vegemite, damper, billy tea, pavlova and pie floaters were seen as the only authentic Australian contributions to world cuisine. Now seekers of a fair-dinkum Aussie dining experience might find themselves joining the Sunday arvo throng in Sydney's Chinatown for 'yum cha'; gorging on bratwurst and sauerkraut in the German-flavoured Adelaide Hills; delighting in a Turkish banquet in Melbourne; or dining out in Hobart on snap-fresh sashimi and sushi.

Australian migrant traditions have endowed the national cuisine with all the above and more – great coffee; every kind of cheese; superb fresh and cured meats; olives and olive oil; and fresh Asian vegies like bok choy and gai larn as well as many fiesty spices. But not all influences have come from foreign shores and good use is made of Australian native or 'bush' foods like wattleseeds, witchetty (wijuti) grubs, macadamia nuts, kangaroo, crocodile and bush tomatoes among the fantastic pickings.

The worldwide, 80s phenomenon of 'nouvelle cuisine' might have made many Austral-

SOUVLAKI CITY

Melbourne has the largest Greek population in Australia. So you shouldn't have any trouble finding souvlaki, taramasalata, ouzo and Greek newspapers in this city.

PIE AN' SAUCE, THANKS

MEAT PIES
These great Aussie hand-held delicacies sit in pie-warmers everywhere – in milkbars, bakeries, highway servos, even some up-market cafes – and are sold by the thousands at sporting events. A day at the footy just wouldn't be the same without chomping through a meat pie with tomato sauce. (It's hard not to eat them quickly, so watch out for second degree burns on the roof of your mouth!) In recent times, pie manufacturers have strayed from the traditional ground beef recipe and you can now get chicken or steak and mushroom and, in some places, more adventurous 'gourmet' types such as beef, spinach and pinenuts, lamb and rosemary or Thai-curried chicken.

TWO NOTABLE AUSSIE PIE EXPERIENCES
- Keep your eyes peeled and your tastebuds primed for the Pie Floater – a species of pie native to South Australia. Quite simply it's a meat pie sitting in a bowl of thick pea soup. Don't be scared; it's actually very tasty, especially on a freezing night or after a night on the booze. Ask anyone on an Adelaide city street for the whereabouts of a pie-cart – they'll point you in the right direction.

- If you find yourself on the highway between Brisbane and the Gold Coast, seek out the turn-off for Yatala (pronounced 'yat-la'), home of the famous Yatala Meat Pie. It'll be one of the most delicious detours you'll ever make! There's a great variety of savoury fare – with or without mashed peas on top; and the pie repertoire also includes some sweet/fruit alternatives. This popular outlet also offers probably the only pie drive-thru service in Australia.

FOOD & DRINK

ian palates more adventurous, but its fleeting popularity was mainly a case of cultural cringe. Australian cuisine is more confident than ever, and you can dine out all over the country every day and never get tired of what's on offer.

MEALS

brekkie
> breakfast. Usually a simple cuppa (tea or coffee) taken with toast, butter and Vegemite, or a rich repast of bacon and eggs (poached, scrambled or fried), or a bowl of muesli or cereal with fresh fruit and yoghurt or milk.

morning tea
> mostly bickies and a cuppa with the occasional indulgence in a cake or bun

brunch
> breakfast and lunch combined, usually a leisurely pastime on the weekends

lunch
> the popular choice is the takeaway sanga (sandwich on white, brown, wholegrain, rye or sourdough bread), foccacia or bagel with an unlimited choice of fillings, but Australians 'do' lunch too: power-broking, networking and socialising at bistros, tavernas, cafes and restaurants

afternoon tea
> try the five-star hotels in the major cities for a luxury treat: freshly brewed tea, petite sandwiches and delightful cakes. Or at any grandma's house: home-made scones, jam and cream, or bickies and tea.

dinner/tea
> the main meal of the day. 'Tea', the Northern English term, is falling out of usage except in rural areas. Sometimes referred to as din-dins, mainly by and for kids.

FOOD & DRINK

BYO

BYO means *Bring Your Own* alcoholic drinks to a restaurant. Choosing a BYO restaurant usually makes eating out more affordable.

FOOD & DRINK

Types of Food

counter meal/tea

a pub meal, not always eaten at the bar, or counter – invariably cheap, and generally along the lines of fish and chips, roasted and grilled meats, or pasta dishes. These hearty meals can also go by the names counter-y and counter-attack.

Devonshire tea

scones with whipped cream and jam and a pot of hot tea. In most country towns you'll stumble across at least one cosy tea (and sometimes twee) room serving this popular fare.

junk food

general term for any kind of food which parents would disapprove of like fried food, pizza, a Mac attack (food from McDonalds, also known as Macka's), lollies and chips. Fried food is also called hot 'n' greasies which mostly refers to fish and chips but can be anything cooked in oil. Another general name for fast food is chew-an'-spew – reflecting a rather jaundiced view perhaps.

munchies

snacks. Chips, pies, chocolate bars and so on would be classed as munchies. To have 'an attack of the munchies' is to suffer sudden severe pangs of hunger, a fate which befalls dope smokers in particular.

nibblies

finger food to nibble on at parties or special do's, like nuts, chips and hors d'oeuvres

nosh

an old-fashioned word for food in general, as in 'Do you feel like some nosh?' In the past people have also eaten chow, grub, and tucker.

a spread

a magnificent offering of food and drink, the veritable groaning board; a spread offers you the chance of a blow-out, bean-feast, or 'pig out'; one result of this approach to eating is the popularity of the 'all-you-can-eat' restaurants, commonly found in the suburbs

AUSSIE TERMS FOR TUCKER

battered sav	saveloy in batter. Sometimes dagwood dog or in SA dippy dog.
bubble & squeak	leftover vegetables, mashed and fried
Chiko roll	a deep-fried bigger cousin of the Chinese spring/egg roll born in the 70s; available at fish and chip shops
coconut ice	type of confectionery; pink and white blocks of desiccated coconut and sugar. Be warned – it's very sweet.
flake	fillet of shark, a popular choice in fish and chip shops
hedgehog	a chocolate-flavoured slice using crushed Arrowroot biscuits (see page 86)
minimum chips	the standard serving of chips available in a fish and chip shop
pav	pavlova; a traditional Australian meringue and cream dessert, named after the ballerina Anna Pavlova (see page 85)

FOOD & DRINK

PEACH MELBA

Anna Pavlova wasn't the only woman honoured with a dessert – the Australian-born opera singer Dame Nellie Melba was the inspiration behind the Peach Melba. This sweet concoction of chilled sponge cake soaked in peach syrup and sherry topped with icecream, almonds and raspberry purée continues to be a hit in some home kitchens. It's a shame Dame Melba's comments about the accent of her fellow Aussies were never as sweet as her namesake dessert!

sausage roll	sausage meat – sometimes spicy – wrapped in flaky pastry. You'll find these snag rolls nestled between meat pies and pasties in pie-warmers across the nation.
scones	these plain, doughy cakes are called 'biscuits' in the USA (see Devonshire tea)
silverbeet	also known as (Swiss) chard
spag bog/bol	spaghetti bolognese. You may hear this dish referred to as spaghetti blow-your-nose

barra	barramundi (fish)
bickies	biscuits
brown bread	wholemeal bread
caulie	cauliflower
cheese and greens	cheese platter
chook	chicken
cut lunch	sandwiches
dead horse	tomato sauce
dodger	bread
dog's eye	meat pie
drumstick	chicken leg
golden syrup	sugar cane syrup
marge	margarine
muddie	mud crab (Qld)
muesli	granola
mushies	mushrooms
'nana	banana
pikelets	little pancakes
sammie	sandwich
spud/'tater	potato
strawbs	strawberries
sweets	dessert
tucker	food
yum cha	dimsum

THEY MAY SAY ...

Not content with just using the word 'egg', Aussies have hatched a few new terms:

bum-nuts
cackleberries
googies/googs
(the 'oo' sound as in 'put')
henfruits

And as for milk ...
cow juice
moo juice

And sausages ...
bangers
snags
mystery bags
snarlers
snorkers

CLASSIC AUSSIE RECIPES

DAMPER
500g flour
1 ½ teaspoons salt
water

Method:
Put flour and salt in a bowl.
Add 3 tablespoons of water and mix.
You may need to add more water.
Form the dough into a ball then flatten into a
thick round of about 60mm.
Place the damper among the hot coals of an open fire –
ensuring that the dough is covered by coal too – and bake for
about 30 minutes.
You can wrap the damper in alfoil prior to baking if you have
an aversion to ash covered damper.
Serve immediately with butter.
If cooking in a home oven, bake at 180°C (350°F) for 30
minutes.

Another way to use damper dough in the bush is to wrap some
around a stick, cook it in the coal and then smother it with
golden syrup (cocky's joy).

PAVLOVA
4 egg whites
pinch salt
250g castor sugar
1 teaspoon white vinegar
1 dessertspoon cornflour

Method:
Beat egg whites until stiff (can form peaks).
Add salt then gradually add sugar.
Add vinegar, beat in well.
Fold in sifted cornflour.
Bake in oven for 30 minutes at 120°C.
Turn off oven and leave in oven for 45 minutes.
When cool, fill with whipped cream and decorate with strawberries, kiwifruit, passionfruit or sliced banana.

FOOD & DRINK

CLASSIC AUSSIE RECIPES

HEDGEHOG
300g butter
11/4 cups castor sugar
3/4 cup cocoa
3 eggs
2 packets of Arrowroot or Marie biscuits
1 cup walnuts
For chocolate coating:
300g dark chocolate buttons
65ml vegetable oil

Method:
Melt butter, then add cocoa and sugar.
Stir well on a gentle heat until sugar's dissolved.
Remove from the heat and cool.
Beat eggs one-by-one into the butter mixture,
then add nuts and coarsely crushed biscuits.
Line a 2cm-deep baking tray with plastic wrap
and press the mixture into it.
Cover with more wrap and put in the fridge for about an hour.
Chocolate coating:
Melt the oil and chocolate over a low heat;
spread a layer over the hedgehog.
Refrigerate for a further 30 minutes, then slice into rectangles.

PUMPKIN SCONES
2 cups self-raising flour
½ teaspoon salt
60g butter
½ tablespoon sugar
1 cup cooked pumpkin, mashed

Method:
After adding butter and sugar to the sifted flour and salt,
rub the ingredients until it looks like breadcrumbs.
Add the pumpkin, stirring lightly until a soft dough forms.
If the dough is too dry and still crumbly,
add a little milk working it in lightly with a fork.
Gently turn the dough out on a floured board.
Pat the dough out until about 2.5cm thick. Cut into rounds.
Grease or butter a baking tray.
Place the scones side by side on the tray
and bake at 220°C for 15-20 minutes.

CLASSIC AUSSIE RECIPES

ANZAC BISCUITS
1 cup plain flour
1 cup rolled oats
3/4 cup desiccated coconut
3/4 cup sugar
125g butter
2 tablespoons golden syrup
1/2 teaspoon bicarbonate of soda
1 tablespoon boiling water

Method:
Mix the sifted flour, oats, coconut and sugar.
Combine butter and syrup, stir over low heat until melted.
Combine the bicarbonate of soda and hot water
and add to the melted butter mixture.
Stir in the dry ingredients and mix well.
Put teaspoon-size balls of the mixture on a lightly
greased oven tray, allow room for spreading.
Bake at 150°C (300°F) for 20 minutes.
Loosen on trays while warm, then allow to cool.
Makes about 35 bickies.

LAMINGTONS
Bake or buy a basic sponge cake.
Make sure that it's square or rectangular.
Cut the cake into blocks and ice all sides with the frosting.
Roll in desiccated coconut.
Allow to dry on wire rack.

Frosting
2 cups icing sugar
1 tablespoon boiling water
1 tablespoon vanilla essence
2 tablespoons cocoa

Method:
Sift icing sugar into a bowl.
Add boiling water and vanilla essence to cocoa.
Stir cocoa mixture into icing sugar and mix well.

FOOD & DRINK

Vegemite & Other Household Names

There are some food items which have become such a part of the Australian way of life that Australians would starve to death without them.

Aeroplane jelly
comes in pretty packets and now in a range of flavours such as tropical, mango and Australian 'lillypilly'. Also has a very popular jingle: 'I like Aeroplane jelly, Aeroplane jelly for me!'

Arnotts arrowroot biscuits
a plain sweet biscuit which is the starting point for a number of desserts or confections, like hedgehog

Coon cheese
a kind of basic cheddar or 'tasty' cheese; nothing to do with the 'coon' of American English

Iced Vo-Vo
a sweet biscuit topped with jam, marshmallow and coconut

Sao biscuits
a large water biscuit, usually smothered in butter and Vegemite, or served with Coon cheese

Tim Tam
one of Australia's favourite biscuits, the Tim Tam has a layer of chocolate cream between two biscuits then covered with milk chocolate

Vegemite
not a chocolate spread but a salty, vitamin-rich yeast extract in the same family as Promite and Marmite. It's spread on toast or dry biscuits like Sao. Some people like their Vegemite spread thinly, others like it in little dabs, and others like it spread thickly – it depends on the level of addiction and the salt threshold of your upper palate. A famous advertising jingle has given rise to the expression 'happy little Vegemites' which refers to contented and well-behaved little children of the kind appearing in the TV ad.

Violet Crumble
a popular chocolate bar consisting of honeycomb covered in chocolate

Childrens' Party Food

chocolate crackles	balls of puffed rice mixed with chocolate and coconut
cordial	any non-aerated soft drink
fairy bread	buttered bread sprinkled with hundreds and thousands
fairy floss	known as 'candy floss' in other countries, and found at fairs
icy pole	frozen flavoured water on a stick
little boys; cheerios	cocktail frankfurts
lollies	confectionary/sweets
lolly water	any aerated soft drink
soft drink	any non-alcoholic drink

THEY MAY SAY ...

Aussies have many expressions to cope with all situations relating to hunger and thirst.

Hunger

> I wouldn't mind a bite
> how about a quick bite
> he's got hollow legs
> I could eat a horse and chase the jockey
> my stomach thinks my throat's cut
> I've got the munchies

Thirst

> I've got a thirst you could photograph
> how about whetting your whistle
> what about a drop, mate
> your tongue's hanging out

The Second Drink

> I could go another one
> how about anotherie?
> that one didn't touch the sides

FOOD & DRINK

CAFE SOCIETY

If it weren't for the great post-war wave of Italian migration, Australians might still be making coffee out of bottled essence, or instant powder. Nowadays no city restaurant (let alone cafe) could make do without its steam-driven espresso machine cranking out well-made cups of java pressed from freshly-ground beans. So important has the cup of coffee become in the modern Australian lifestyle that rising real estate prices can be tracked merely by counting the number of espresso machines per head in any given city suburb. And god help you if you're out to impress and you don't know your latte from your macchiato.

Unless you're travelling only in rural areas, where the choice in (instant) coffee will probably be limited to 'black or white, love?', you've got to know your (bean) stuff. Here are some of the more usual brews:

caffe latte (or just 'latte')
 1/2 espresso, 1/2 steamed milk: slightly frothy and served in a glass

flat white
 2/3 espresso, 1/3 steamed milk: no froth hence the word 'flat'. Usually served in a cup, if only to distinguish it from a latte.

short black
 small espresso, particularly strong

long black
 order this if you've got the caff-crave for a basic black espresso coffee

macchiato (long or short 'mac')
 an espresso or a long black with, as the word 'macchiato' translates, just a 'stain' of cold milk

CAFE SOCIETY

double espresso
the post business-lunch power jolt: two espresso shots in the one cup

cappuccino (or just 'capp')
1/3 espresso with 1/3 steamed milk and 1/3 milk froth, usually topped with sprinkled chocolate powder. Don't be alarmed if your capp arrives without the chokkie – it just means you're sitting in one of the cafes following a new trend of serving cappuccinos as the Italians do.

skinny capp/latte
variations with low fat, or 'skinny' milk

baby-cino
milk froth in a tiny cup, topped with sprinkled chocolate powder; cafe society training-wheels for kids

soya-cino
cappuccino made with soy milk instead of cow's milk

ecco-cino
a de-caf cappuccino using Ecco, a powder made of roasted barley herbs that tastes like coffee

decaf ... (latte, capp, etc)
any coffee made with decaffeinated coffee beans. Before you order, remember the restaurant scene from Steve Martin's film *LA Story*.

vienna coffee
black coffee with a blob of whipped cream

white coffee
coffee served with milk already in it; this term is used when there's no espresso machine in sight

Virtually no-one in Australia orders anything with a 'twist' of lemon. If you must, order a 'slice'.

FOOD & DRINK

FOOD & DRINK

FRUITY FESTIVALS

If you're an aficionado of fruit, make sure you're in Coominya, Queensland for the annual Grape and Watermelon Festival. Held on the second Saturday in January, this country fruitfest will show you a world of watermelons and grapes beyond the fruit salad bowl. See the fruits' versatility as they're scoffed, thrown, rolled, judged, relayed in races and, in the case of the melons, carried across the finish line in the 20kg Watermelon Marathon. The Seed Spitting Challenge, bush dance, street parade and arts and crafts make this a wonderful food festival with a twist!

Not subjected to quite the same athletic demands are the mangoes honoured at the Mango Festival in Broome, WA. For one weekend in November, the town is gripped by mango fever as it celebrates the existence of this sublime tropical fruit. The festival features mango wine-tasting sessions, mango-eating contests, mango cocktail parties, a mango mardi gras and other mango madness.

Murwillumbah is a sleepy hollow in the Tweed Valley; but every August it explodes with banana-mania during the Tweed Valley Banana Festival and Harvest Week. Although the festival was launched in the 1950s as the town's way to hail their banana industry, it has grown into a major festival with open air rock concerts, pistol shoots, art and quilt exhibitions, fashion parades and other non-banana themed events. But if you're seeking some banana fun, there are also banana sporting events, banana eating opportunities and the crowning of the many Banana Monarchs – King Banana, Queen Banana and the little Banana Princesses, all of whom do the royal wave, perched on their floats for the final street parade.

BEER

As a rule each state remains fiercely loyal to their local beers – most pubs only have the state champion on tap. Whether it's VB (Victoria Bitter) in Victoria, Swan in WA, XXXX ('fourex') in Queensland or West End in SA, the irony is that they really don't taste all that different. Lager is the dominant style, served ice-cold; a bottle of beer is sometimes just called a coldie, as in 'Jeez, I could handle a coldie right now'.

In the late 80s 'boutique' breweries sprouted across the country, often in pubs with a microbrewery attached. Most concentrate on European stouts, ales and pilseners rather than competing head-on with the giant lager manufacturers. Even so, in a country pub you may find the choice is Brand X or Brand Y, both always made by CUB, Tooheys, or Castlemaine.

Recently Irish pub franchises have been springing up in the major cities, and while they tend to be far larger than their Dublin templates they have a certain transplanted charm. Pints

FOOD & DRINK

of Harp Lager, Newcastle Brown Ale and – no surprises here – Guinness are available at prices that can shock the natives but are on a par with the British Isles.

While most Australians agree on drinking beer, the different states have different ideas on how to go about doing it. Here's a short guide to some of the terms related to beer drinking:

BOTTLE-O

DRINK IN

bobby	6 oz glass in WA
butcher	6 oz glass in SA
glass	5 oz glass in WA
handle	medium-sized beer glass with a handle
middy	10 oz glass in NSW/Qld; 7 oz glass in WA
pot	10 oz glass in WA/Vic/Qld
schooner	15 oz glass in NSW/Qld; 9 oz glass in SA
ten	10 oz glass of beer in NT (you can also order a fifteen)

TAKE AWAY

Darwin stubby	humungous beer bottle, reputedly the largest in the world at 75oz (2.25 Lt)
dead marine	an empty beer bottle
echo	small beer bottle in SA
stubbie	small beer bottle
tallie	large bottle of beer
tinnie	a tin of beer – also called a tube
nine	a nine-gallon beer keg
eighteen	an 18-gallon beer keg
beer	lager in Victoria; a pot of beer gets you a glass of lager
grog	general term for beer or spirits

Pubs

It's important to know where to sample Aussie beer with all it's different styles and sizes and a pub is the best place to start. A pub can be anything from a small bush shanty with bar and verandah to a glossy, groovy city number. If it's close to home and a favoured haunt then it's known as **the local**; other petnames include **the rubbidy** (rhyming slang, 'rubbidy dub' means 'pub'), **the pisser** or **the boozer**. Most pubs have a **bottleshop** (bottle-o in SA) to sell beer, wine, etc, to takeaway and is often a drive-thru service; but there are other **bottleshops** which operate independently of pubs.

WINE

Australian table wines have gone from being a national joke to a multi-billion dollar industry in barely 30 years, and the upsurge of new wineries and vineyards continues. Australia now rates as either the 10th or 11th biggest winemaking country, and Australians are the biggest wine drinkers in the English-speaking world.

Before the 70s, table wines weren't popular, and sherry and port ruled supreme. The Australian table wine exports in the wine industry's infancy earned a terrible reputation with brands such as Wallaby White and Kanga Rouge, which allegedly made even the cheapest Spanish **plonk** seem like Beaujolais by comparison. Although not as fashionable these days, fortified wines such as the ports, muscats and tokays of Rutherglen in northeastern Victoria can be superb and reasonably priced.

Winemakers tend to concentrate on single-variety wines such as the ubiquitous Chardonnay or simple blends such as Cabernet Sauvignon and Merlot, rather that the more blended and structured European style of winemaking. The basic aim is to preserve as much of the fruit character as possible.

Vineyards and wineries tend to be within a day's drive of the southern capitals, reflecting the phenomenon of city-based professionals wanting to own vineyards not too far from the office. Some of the more highly regarded areas include the Barossa and

TEN WINES TO TRY

- Hunter Valley Semillon
- Rutherglen Port
- Coonawarra Cabernet Sauvignon
- Central Victorian Shiraz
- Adelaide Hills Chardonnay
- Sparkling Burgundy
- Yarra Valley Methode Champenoise
- Albany Pinor Noir
- Clare Valley Rhine Riesling
- Barossa Valley dryland Shiraz

Clare Valleys, Southern Vales, Coonawarra and Adelaide Hills in South Australia, Margaret River and Albany in Western Australia, the Mornington Peninsula, Yarra Valley and Pyrenees in Victoria, and the Hunter Valley, Mudgee and Canberra areas in NSW and the ACT. In Tasmania the region north of Launceston has a great reputation for sparkling wines. Even Queensland rates with the high-altitude Granite Belt on the NSW border.

bin
   a term from the stock-keeping system of the Penfolds group, sometimes seen on labels, i.e. Bin 707
BYO
   Bring Your Own; Australian licensing laws allow diners to bring their own alcohol to restaurants not licensed to sell alcohol
Cab Sav
   Cabernet Sauvignon
Cab Merl
   Cabernet Sauvignon and Merlot
cask wine
   typically cheap and cheerful wine sold in a cardboard box with a plastic bladder inside. This Australian invention is sometimes called chateau cardboard

corkage
> the fee charged by restaurants for BYO wines, usually around $1.50 per person

dryland
> unirrigated vineyards

Grange Hermitage
> the nation's top-quality red, created by a brilliant but chain-smoking winemaker Max Schubert who wanted a wine he could taste

Moselle
> your basic white wine, usually sold in casks. The term was 'borrowed' from Europe, along with sherry, port, claret, hermitage and, 10 years, ago, even champagne.

Muscat Gordo Blanco
> Muscat of Alexandria

preservative 220
> sulphur, which is added to bins of grapes to prevent them spoiling on the way to being crushed at a winery

plonk
> cheap wine also called bombo, red ned and steam

Sparkling Burgundy
> red champagne; an Australian speciality

Southcorp
> the dominant company in the industry, encompassing brands such as Seppelts, Penfolds, Seaview, Kaiser Stuhl and dozens of others

sparkling wine
> slang terms include shampoo, wa-wa juice, fizz and le pop

Rhine Riesling
> Riesling

Riverland
> the irrigation belt along the Murray River, producer of much of Australia's cheap bulk wines

Shiraz
> Syrah

vino
> general term for wine

GROGGING ON

booze bus
    police van used for random breath testing for
    alcohol
grog on
    to drink alcohol over quite a long period of time
heart starter
    an alcoholic drink usually in the morning
leg opener
    alcoholic drink calculated to assist in the
    seduction of a woman
liquid amber
    general term for beer; also called slops or suds
on the turps
    currently in the habit of drinking vast amounts
    of alcohol
shout
    to buy a round of drinks in a pub
tides gone out
    your glass is empty – it's time for another beer!

alkie	an alcoholic
bevvie	beverage; refers to a beer
coldie	cold bottle or can of beer
frostie	cold bottle or can of beer
tinnie	can of beer

drink with the flies	to drink alone
duck's dinner	drinking with nothing to eat
hair of the dog	strong alcohol – taken to cure a hangover
pig's ear	beer
pub crawl	bar hopping
put on the wobbly boot	to get drunk
sit on a beer	to drink a beer slowly
sherbet	alcoholic beverage
wally grout	shout

FOOD & DRINK

THE AUSSIE PARTY

THE CLASSIC AUSSIE PARTY

The party – otherwise known as 'a bit of a bash' among older Australians – is central to the Australian expectation of having a good time in life. These days, the average urban party-goer may well be spotted in the traditional place alongside the barbecue (especially if male) and wearing a T-shirt and shorts. However, he or she may be 'knocking back the chilled chardonnay' rather than the old-fashioned tinnie, and conversation will focus on the latest arty film as often as the footy results. The time-honoured rituals described below survive mostly in conservative social groups.

First of all everyone drinks and talks – this is the warming up. In the old days the men talked to the men (about sport mainly) and the women talked to the women (about clothes and children). A few party games help to relax everyone – these can be as simple as chasing people to put ice down their backs or as complicated as a game of pool. The midnight swim is still a favourite – on the beach or in the pool. At some stage in the evening the 'boys will become the boys' and do silly things like throwing rocks on the roof of the neighbour's house to wake them up or attempt to drive the car onto the roof for a better view. They'll also turn the music up very loud. The police might be called and possibly, in the most successful parties, the fire brigade. There's not much that one can do with the police but the fire brigade has been known to pose for party pictures. The women will take command and hush and shush the boys until they promise to behave. Eventually they'll collapse into sleep now that the high point of the party has been achieved.

> ### PARTY FRIDGE
>
> It's common to find the bath full of ice during parties. If you're happy to share your favourite drop and sample some others put it there to chill, if not keep it safely under your arm.

Bit of a Bash

You may find that you're invited to a strange event and get there to find it's just an Aussie party.

- party
  bit of a bash; shindig; rage; beano; wing-ding; piss-up; booze-up; shivoo

- conversation
  small talk; chit-chat; rap; bit of a yarn (especially among older men); gossip session; a wongi; d and m ('deep and meaningful' conversation)

- to chat
  bat the breeze; chew the fat/rag; have a natter (older females, or men describing their way of talking)

Drinking Protocol

The best approach is to go immediately to the bottle shop and buy whatever poison takes your fancy. This isn't a suggestion that suicide might be preferable to what follows. Poison is drink – alcoholic drink. Most commonly people go to the party armed with tinnies which can be purchased in a slab (a carton of 24 beer cans), or opt for the trusty cask of plonk (cheap wine, red or white). On arrival at the party a rosiner will be suggested – one to whet your whistle. Notice will have been given either verbally or in writing that the party is BYO (sometimes BYOG) – 'Bring Your Own (Grog)'. Sometimes barbecues will be labelled BYOGM – 'Bring Your Own Grog and Meat'. The host will then provide the extras.

Nibblies Protocol

If people are asked to bring a plate to a party, function or barbecue ('Ladies, please bring a plate'), this means they're requested to bring a plate of food to be shared with all the other attendees at the same event, not just an empty plate! This food is often in the form of cakes, slices or biscuits, but it also can extend to savoury dishes such as casseroles, pies or sausage rolls, and even dips, breads and other nibblies. The host(s) or organisers will sometimes try to nominate what 'type' of plate to bring.

JOYRIDING THE PORCELAIN BUS!

THE ARGUMENT

A party-goer may have a bit of a barney (old-fashioned word for argument) with someone, which usually sets out to be of the friendly good-humoured variety but in some cases can take a serious turn. Most often the friendly arguments are about sport, even politics. There's a wide range of useful words (see below) that can be applied to the opposition which are acceptable as long as the basic intention is amiable and they're uttered with a reassuring smile.

boofhead
  possibly derived from a 16th century word 'buffle' for a fool, which was a borrowed French term of abuse (in French it means 'buffalo')
you great galah
  galahs have a bad reputation in Australia for being noisy, gregarious, and stupid
dumbcluck
  this draws on the well-known idiocy of chickens
nincompoop
  someone has suggested that this is related to 'non compos (mentis)' but no-one really knows
bloody drongo
  Drongo was a horse that insisted on coming second in all its races rather than first

THE AUSSIE PARTY

DID YOU KNOW ... There's a story that dinkum (see page 105) is a Chinese word meaning 'real gold' and refers to the anxieties of the goldfields when distinguishing real from false gold was an issue, but this is apparently folklore.

RACK OFF, HAIRY LEGS!

lose one's temper	spit the dummy; blow a fuse; lose one's cool; blow one's stack or top; chuck a wobbly; cut up rough; do one's block or nana; flip one's lid; go off one's brain; go through the roof; go nuts or bonkers; chuck a mental; spit chips; get off one's bike; crack the shits
argument	bit of a barney; bust-up; ding or wing-ding; set-to; argy-bargy
angry	fit to be tied; foaming at the mouth; hot under the collar; off one's face; ropeable; aggro; burr up
cross with someone	dark on someone; dirty on someone; miffed; shirty; snakey; sore; narked on someone
in a bad mood	browned off; cheesed off; fed up to the back teeth; have the shits; pissed off; snitchy; uptight; ticked off
crazy or stupid	silly as a two-bob watch; not the full quid; has gone troppo; the lift doesn't go to the top floor; lame-brained; basketcase
idiot	imbo (short for 'imbecile'); a mug alec; a nerd; dork; dickhead; nong; wombat; alf; wacker; goose; rabbit
to abuse	bore it up someone; get stuck into someone; give someone a blast; give someone heaps; tip the bucket on someone
to fight	to mix it with someone; come to blows; go the knuckle; stack on a turn; bash up

RACK OFF, HAIRY LEGS!

a fight	a blue; a box-on; a bust-up; barney; dust up; go-in; a rough-house; set-to; donnybrook; free-for-all; punch-up; run-in; yike
to become scared	go to water; pack shit; pack death; take a willy; chicken out; pike out; show the white feather
coward	a gutless wonder; a damp squib; dingo; nervous Nellie; scaredy-cat; sook; wimp; yellow-belly; piker; poofter; sheila; wuss
be in trouble	the shit hits the fan; be in more strife than Ned Kelly (Australian bushranger hanged in 1880); up shit creek
'get stuffed!'	Get a rat up ya!; Get a big black dog up ya!; Rack off (hairy legs)!; Get knotted!; Bite ya bum!
to tease	chiack; razz someone; stir; send someone up; take the mickey out of someone

THE 'BAD GUYS'

Among the guests at the party will be the inevitable bullshit artist, the con man who wants to confide to someone his latest lurk or rort To rort the system is to twist the rules or procedures of an organisation in a manner which is either illegal or bordering on illegality, for one's own advantage. This used to be an activity popularly thought to be a political specialty but has spread now that many Australians realise it's quite a good idea. Rorts are also known as scams or shonks

bludger
> person who lives off other people, either financially or emotionally

cadger
> like a bludger, a bloodsucker or parasite

yobbos or yobs
> uncouth, aggressive people with no subtlety to their antisocial behaviour

dobber
> person who reports a scam, rort, bludger, etc (also disliked)

Foul Play

- cadge   put the bite on; put the fangs into; bot; bludge; fang; put the hard word on; sting; touch; put the nips into

- scheme   rort; scam; shonk; dodge; hum; sting; touch

THE 'GOOD GUYS'

fair dinkum
> Genuine; cannot be faulted; the truth. This expression comes from Lancashire dialect and refers to the basic notion that a fair day's work (or dinkum) demands a fair day's pay.

good sport
> People, men or women, who have never played sport let along a team sport in their lives can still be described as good sports. It's one of the highest accolades. A good sport is good-natured and uncomplaining, accepts chiacking cheerfully, and is willing to give something or someone a go.

tall poppy
> A tall poppy is an achiever. Knockers (critics) will always want to cut them down. The tall poppy syndrome, a tendency to criticize anyone who's gained fame or fortune, is a 'disease' afflicting many Australians.

THE AUSSIE PARTY

Fair Dealing

- **deal honestly** — play it straight; play with a straight bat; play fair; lay it on the line

- **truth** — the good oil; the drum; the full two bob; the good guts; the griff; the real thing; the straight wire; true dinks

- **honest person** — plain-dealer; square-shooter; straight talker

- **honest** — up-front; above board; dinky-di; straight up and down; ridgy-didge

PISSED AS A FART

drunk	blotto tanked plastered faceless sozzled shickered pickled legless rat-arsed primed	pissed to the eyeballs sloshed tight as a tick stewed to the gills full as a goog/boot drunk as a skunk rotton as a chop pissed out of your brain pissed as a fart/newt/ parrot
drugged	off the planet high bombed loaded stoked spacey	off one's face stoned smashed ripped spaced out high as a kite
throw up	chunder spew ralph hurl	drive the porcelain bus do a technicolour yawn chunderspew blow chunks

LEAVING THE PARTY

On leaving, the usual expressions include: Cheerio, you say, I'm going to choof (off) now; shoot through like a Bondi tram; chuck it in for the night.

Those who can still talk the next day can admit to a hangover with symptoms described as the horrors, the Joe Blakes (shakes), the DTs, blue devils, pink elephants and dingbats. This isn't to say that the sufferer is a heavy drinker or a:

booze artist
hard case
alkie
lush
grog artist
pisshead
pisspot
soak
boozehound
sponge

THEY MAY SAY ...

paralytic/para
inebriated

In Melbourne you may hear the phrase para by the Yarra to describe a drunken barbie on the banks of the Yarra River.

Some indeed may be two-pot screamers – totally off their heads after just two drinks of beer.

NIGHTLIFE
Clubs & Pubs

There are plenty of 'clubs' in country and suburban areas around which the social life of a community revolves. Such watering holes include sporting clubs, most notably football clubs which have associated football teams and offer extensive drinking and gambling facilities; and RSL (Returned Servicemen's League) clubs, affectionately known as the Rozzer, where you may be asked to be silent for a minute in honour of fallen Australian soldiers. However, in the bigger cities a 'club' is a nightclub to which punters go as late as possible – after having kickstarted the night off in a bar or cafe – to drink and dance often until the

DRINKING WITH CHLOE

Chloe is a nude in a painting that hangs on the wall of Young & Jackson's bar in Melbourne and inspired the phrase drunk as Chloe.

sun comes up. Australian liquor licensing laws mean that if you really wanted to you could start out on Friday, get home on Monday, and never have stopped dancing, drinking or socialising in between. Take your pick: cosy blues bar, multi-level dance club (maybe hip-hop up the top, hardcore trance in the middle, luvved-up house down below), 70s or 80s music themed nights at dance venues or loungey, laid-back grooves at a fashionable hideaway.

A lot of night – and day – life centres on the pub (especially in country towns) where families will come early for a counter meal; others will linger with some mates and a beer or six; play darts or shoot some pool (many pubs have pool teams and regular tournaments); or tune into some live rock 'n' roll.

Cinema

Cinema is enormously popular both in the cities and in country towns, where it's still occasionally called the flicks. As Australians are ranked among the biggest cinema-goers in the world with ticket sales increasing every year, there's no shortage of cinemas and films for your viewing pleasure. Small 'arthouse' cinemas show foreign-language and avant-garde films, while large companies like Hoyts and Village compete to show the blockbusters and big names. During the summer months, Moonlight Cinemas are becoming more popular – you can catch a film under the stars as you lounge on a picnic blanket. Country cinemas will usually only offer the latest from Hollywood. It's worth noting that in most cities there are cinemas that offer a 'cheap night', selling tickets to all films at almost half the usual price: generally it's either Monday or Tuesday.

Arts Scene

All of Australia's major cities have thriving arts scenes, and even the smallest country towns will have a repertory theatre group and a gallery of some sort. Check newspapers for art and photography exhibitions, theatre, comedy shows, concerts, dance and opera, all of which Australians flock to in the thousands. It'll be an extremely rare week (or even day) that you're in Australia and there's *not* a major festival of the arts being staged (see page 114).

FESTIVALS

Australians love parties – they also love festivals and there are hundreds to choose from. Here are just a small handful of some of the bigger celebrations.

Australia Day

On January 26, Australia commemorates the landing of the First Fleet in 1788 by a national holiday, lively concerts and the announcement of the Australia Day Awards, including the award for the Australian of The Year.

Australasian Country Music Festival

Yeehah! Tamworth is Australia's Country Music Capital and each January, guitars, voices and award ceremonies are in full swing entertaining the eager, boot tappin' throngs! Find a good perch on Peel Street when the cavalcade of floats, bands and record-breaking line-dancers (last count was one continuous line of 5,502 people!)

GO COCKIE, GO!

If you're in Darwin on Australia Day, you may want to see the **Cockroach Race**. Pick a favourite 'roach and cheer it on as it scrambles as fast as its many legs will carry it, through plastic tubing in the shape of Australia.

THE AUSSIE PARTY

ANZAC DAY

Each year, 25 April marks the first landing of Australian troops (diggers) at Gallipoli in 1915. Memorial marches are held all over Australia to remember and honour the more than 102,000 Australians who died during all wars, as well as the many veterans who returned after having bravely served their country.

move through the town for the parade celebrating country music. Rodeos are also a big feature with cowboys and cowgirls vying for victory in such events as Bareback Bronco Riding and Steer Wrestling. The 10-day festival is a wonderful experience for everyone, not only country music fans.

Sydney Gay & Lesbian Mardi Gras

Not just a famously spectacular parade and an all-night dance party in Oxford Street, this month-long festival in February also features theatre, art, photography and music in a celebration of gay and lesbian life.

Moomba

Running for two weeks in March, this fun-filled summer festival in Melbourne ends with a street parade reigned over by a Moomba Monarch, usually a popular TV or sporting personality. The word 'moomba' was chosen as it was thought to mean 'let's get together and have fun' in an Aboriginal language. In fact, a more accurate translation would be the slightly inappropriate 'bottom/bum'.

Port Fairy Folk Festival

This usually low-key coastal town in Victoria welcomes a deluge of folk music fans every Labour Day weekend in March. As well as around 40 concerts, the festival also presents a

THE AUSSIE PARTY

jampacked program of storytelling, music classes and singalongs, dancing, a food festival, street markets, performances and parades, the Children's Folk Circus and numerous workshops. It's the largest folk music festival in Australia and is extremely popular.

Torres Strait Cultural Festival

In May of each year, Thursday Island hosts the Torres Stait Cultural Festival. This is designed to promote and strengthen cultural identity. The activities of the Cultural Festival include traditional dance, traditional and contemporary singing, and stalls where people sell food, handicrafts, artefacts and carvings of all description.

Barunga Sports & Cultural Festival

Attracting about 40 Aboriginal groups from all over the Northern Territory, this festival is a great place to experience some Aboriginal culture. There are plenty of traditional arts and crafts exhibits, native dancing and music including the hypnotic sounds of the didgeridoo; as well as sporting competitions like spearthrowing, boomeranging and firelighting. It's a good opportunity to sample native Australian bush tucker too – honey ants, kangaroo tail soup, witchetty (witjuti) grubs and roasted possom, snake and goanna (lizard). This wonderful gathering is in Barunga, 80kms southeast of Katherine, in early June.

B & S BALLS

Bachelor & Spinster Balls – held in big tents and shearing sheds all over Australia – attract the young and thirsty in their thousands. Alcohol is skulled in mind-blowing amounts by bachelors in black tie and spinsters in taffeta gowns as they dance, roll around in the well-trodden mud and throw food dye (!) at each other. Some even find a partner at these traditional Aussie events!

THE AUSSIE PARTY

THE AUSSIE PARTY

Beer Can Regatta

This rowdy occasion in July/August is a 'sailing' race at Mindil Beach in Darwin between 'boats' built with empty beer cans. Half the fun for the competitors and their friends, in this city of enthusiastic drinkers, is *emptying* the beer cans. For those that prefer activities on terra firma, there are bottomless boat races on sand, thong-throwing show-downs, bathing beauty contests and so much more.

BEANIE BEANO

Alice Springs jumps to the beat of the **Beanie Festival** in early July when it celebrates this popular winter head-dress. One of the big drawcards is the competition giving prizes for 'the craziest beanie', 'the best made beanie', etc. You'll also find local beanie-topped models strutting down a catwalk, and a workshop for keen beanie makers.

Shinju Matsuri (Festival of the Pearl)

For 10 days in September, the port town of Broome comes alive as it celebrates its pearling history and diverse cultural heritage. This colourful festival is launched by a traditional opening ball and finishes with a beach concert – 'Opera-under-the-stars' – and a brilliant fireworks display; other highlights include a float parade, pearl jewellery and art exhibitions, the must-see dragon boat races, traditional Japanese ceremonies and the Carnival of Nations.

Henley-on-Todd Regatta & Beerfest

A boat race on a dry river bed? Head for Alice Springs in late September to check out the crews 'wearing' their colourful, inventive boat creations as they stir up the dust – bounding for glory down the empty Todd River. Watch out for the **Camel Cup** in July when it's the camels turn (without the seacraft) to compete in the same dry river bed.

Royal Shows

Each city has a Royal Show offering livestock contests, agricultural displays, novelty rides and sideshows. The cake decorating competitions and the showing-off of primped and preened cats and dogs also draw people by the thousands. Hard to resist are the 'showbags' containing 'junk food' fare and other wares from manufacturers around Australia. Here's the place to gobble down fairy floss, toffee apples and dagwood dogs.

March/April	*Royal Easter Show*, Sydney
July	*Royal Shows*, Northern Territory
August	*Royal National Exhibition* (the Ekka), Brisbane
September	*Royal Shows*, Melbourne, Adelaide, Perth

International Film Festivals

These 'celebrations of celluloid' are on offer in each major city and showcase a remarkable array of contemporary films from Australia and around the globe. The festival in Melbourne has long been regarded as the premier filmfest in Australia offering filmbuffs fabulous cinema – and a warm seat during the winter months of July and August.

NATIONAL HOLIDAYS

New Years's Day	1 January
Australia Day	26 January
Easter	Good Friday, Easter Saturday, Sunday and Monday (March/April)
Anzac Day	25 April
Queen's Birthday	2nd Monday in June (not WA)
Queen's Birthday	1st Monday in October (WA only)
Christmas Day	25 December
Boxing Day	26 December

THE AUSSIE PARTY

Arts Festivals

Each major city stages an Arts Festival that acts as a magnet for millions of 'culture vultures' and gives thousands of local and international artists an opportunity to wow these audiences with their talents. On offer is an extraordinary range of opera, dance, drama, comedy, film, music, visual arts, literature, street parades, community events and plenty of parties in between.

DESERT MOB

Every July **The Desert Mob Art Show** at the Araluen Centre in Alice Springs exhibits a diverse range of work from established and emerging Aboriginal artists from all over the Northern Territory, South Australia and Western Australia.

Sydney Festival & Carnivale: *January.*
Kickstarted by the not-to-be-missed fireworks extravaganza above the Harbour Bridge on New Year's Eve.

Festival of Perth: *February/March.*
One of the oldest and largest festivals in the southern hemisphere, this cultural treat is a regular tourist award winner.

Adelaide Arts Festival: *March (biennial).*
Considered by many as the most innovative and well-known of all the Festivals; there's also an excellent 'alternative' arts Fringe Festival.

Warana Festival (Brisbane): *September.*
Meaning 'blue skies' in an Aboriginal language, Warana offers nearly three weeks of artistic events and those of a more rowdy nature like beer festivals, a rodeo and rock concerts.

International Festival of the Arts (Melbourne): *October.*
Formerly the Spoleto Festival, there's always an exciting range of work to marvel at, including a particularly good Fringe Festival.

THE AUSSIE PARTY

The main sports in Australia are footy ('football') and cricket. The term footy, however, refers to different codes of football in different states: mainly Australian Rules in the southern states and Rugby League in New South Wales and Queensland. Soccer is seldom called footy or even 'football' in Australia, much to the confusion of European and South American visitors. Some of the footy teams are household names, as are some of the players.

AUSTRALIAN RULES FOOTBALL

This uniquely Australian sport is mainly played in the southern states, though there's now a national competition. The season runs from March to September, and the game is played on an oval up to 200 metres from end to end with four posts at each end: two inner, taller ones called goal posts, two smaller, outer ones called behind posts. Teams of 18 (plus three interchange-

---

THEY MAY SAY ...

avagoyermug
'have a go, you mug!'. Traditional rallying call, especially at cricket matches.

barrack
to cheer on a team at a sporting event (in some other countries, barracking means 'abusing the opposing team')

caaarn!
typical cry, meaning 'come on', as in 'Caaarn The Cats!'

chewie on ya boot!
a barrackers call aimed at distracting an Aussie Rules footballer on the verge of kicking a goal

able players on each side) aim to kick an oval ball cleanly between the goal posts and score a goal (six points). If the ball is touched on its way, or touches the post, or goes between a goal post and a behind/point post, it's worth a 'behind' (one point). Scores of 20 goals or more by one or both teams are common. There are four quarters of 25 minutes each.

The winning team is the team with the highest number of points at the end of the game, with drawn games being quite rare. Tackling is fierce, with only tackling above the shoulder or round the legs banned. If the ball is kicked and goes through the air for more than 10 metres and is then caught, this is called a mark and the player is awarded a free kick. Throwing the ball is barred, but a hand pass – holding the ball in the palm of one hand and hitting it with a clenched fist – is legal.

The 18 Positions

full back line	two back pockets and one full back
half back line	two half back flankers and one centre half back
centre line	two wingers and one centre man
half forward line	two half forward flankers and one centre half forward
full forward line	two forward pockets and one full forward
ruckman	
ruck rover	
rover	

FAMOUS FOOTY VENUES

the MCG	Melbourne Cricket Ground
Football Park	Adelaide
Subiaco	Perth
WACA	West Australian Cricket Association, Perth
Optus Oval	Melbourne
Waverley Park	Melbourne
Gabba	Brisbane Cricket Ground

Major Annual Events

AFL (Australian Football League) Grand Final, September, attended by almost 100,000 and watched on TV by millions.

Also the presentation of the Brownlow Medal to the player judged best and fairest by the umpires over the whole season.

AFL Teams

Adelaide – the Crows
Brisbane – the Lions
Carlton – the Blues
Collingwood – the Magpies or Pies
Essendon – the Bombers
Fremantle – the Dockers
Geelong – the Cats

Hawthorn – the Hawks
Footscray and surrounding areas – the Western Bulldogs
Melbourne – the Demons or Ds
North Melbourne – the Kangaroos

Perth – the West Coast Eagles
Port Adelaide – Port Power
Richmond – the Tigers
St Kilda – the Saints
Sydney – the Swans

YA DROP KICK

Ball Kicks

There are many ways of kicking the oval-shaped ball:

drop punt; drop kick (out of fashion kick, but in fashion as a term of verbal abuse); torp; screwie; checkside or banana kick; stab pass; mongrel punt; hospital ball; lean back and go bang; set sail for home and a rain maker

Some Aussie Rules Football Identities

Ron Barassi	former Melbourne and Carlton star best known for his highly successful coaching career
Ted Whitten	'Mr Football'; Footscray legend who will always be associated with the Victorian State-of-Origin team and who was given a state funeral

THEY MAY SAY ...

white maggot	umpire
speckie	spectacular high mark
coat hangered	hit by a straight arm
dragged	taken off the field

Kevin Sheedy	highly successful Essendon coach who led the 'Baby Bombers' to the 1993 Premiership
Tom Hafey	famous coach of Richmond and several other clubs
Bob Skilton	star of South Melbourne – now Sydney – and three-time winner of the Brownlow medal
Kevin Bartlett	400-game Richmond veteran
Michael Tuck	400-game Hawthorn veteran
Leigh Matthews	uncompromising Hawthorn star and late Collingwood coach who once snapped off a point post unaided
Lou Richards	former Collingwood rover, captain and identity, known for his short stature and later for his inaccurate tipping; also remembered for his unsavoury 'clash' with Geelong captain Fred Flanigan
Gary Ablett	known as 'God', especially by the adoring Geelong fans; magnificent full-forward who several times topped the goal-kickers' table and won the Norm Smith Medal in the 1989 Grand Final when he kicked nine goals for a losing team
Jason Dunstall	tough, unselfish Hawthorn full-forward who may yet break Gordon Coventry's career goal-kicking record of 1299

Dermott Brereton	flamboyant, mischievous and highly skilled Hawthorn half-forward
Peter Matera	mercurial West Coast winger/half-back who emerged as a major star with five goals and the Norm Smith Medal as his team became the first ever non-Victorian AFL Premiers in 1992
Sam Newman	Geelong star of the 70s and 80s, now a totally unconventional and entertaining TV personality
Robert DiPierdomenico	'Dipper'; star of the great Hawthorn team of the late 1980s, now frequently seen on TV, though not always in a football context
Doug Hawkins	rugged but much loved Footscray champion
Tony Lockett	'Plugger'; best full-forward now playing, having moved from St Kilda to Sydney

RUGBY LEAGUE FOOTBALL

This is the main traditional winter sport in New South Wales and Queensland although Aussie Rules has been making inroads of late. 'League' broke away from rugby union in England in the 1890s, many of the rules changed and it rapidly became semi-professional at top level. It spread to Australia (and New Zealand) by 1908 but isn't as well known around the world as rugby union. The ground with large H-shaped posts at either end, the ball and the general nature of play are similar to union, but most visitors to Australasia will find some details unfamiliar (unless they come from the right part of England!).

There are 13 players on a team (with substitutes); they attempt to get the oval ball past their opponents by hand-passing it (always backwards) or kicking it (usually forwards, but the receiver must run from behind the kicker). Placing the ball on the ground behind the goal-line scores a try (four points) which can then be 'converted' by a place kick through the H and over the bar (two more points). There are also penalty goals (two points again) and field goals (one point). A tackled player regains his feet and heels the ball backwards to a colleague – so there's no rucking/mauling as in rugby union (after six tackles the other team gets possession unless the ball goes dead).

The dominant teams are Brisbane, Canberra, Newcastle and Sydney teams such as Manly, Canterbury and St George. Melbourne recently got a pro club for the first time.

The Positions

Seven backs (one full-back, four three-quarter backs, one five-eighth, one half-back) and six forwards.

Major Events

Most big matches (including the big finals in September, culminating in the Grand Final) are played in Sydney and Brisbane. Each year New South Wales and Queensland teams are selected to meet in the three 'State of Origin' matches: rugby league at its best. Australia's recent domination of world rugby league has meant that international matches haven't been up to the same standard for a while, but Great Britain and New Zealand do still manage to beat the Kangaroos in a match from time to time.

Some Rugby League Identities

Wally Lewis	flamboyant and amazingly skilful five-eighth and hugely successful captain of Brisbane, Queensland and Australia
Mal Meninga	magnificent centre. Captain of Queensland and Australia. Beloved star of the Canberra Raiders.
John 'Chicka' Ferguson	hero of Canberra's epic 1989 Grand Final win over Balmain despite his advanced age
Paul 'Fatty' Vautin	the archetype of a forward surprisingly fast and skilful given his bulk, a star for Manly
Peter Sterling	'Sterlo'; greatest scrum-half of recent years. Superstar for Parramatta, NSW and Australia.

SPORTS

RUGBY UNION FOOTBALL

Rugby union is the older code of rugby – in Australia it's often called just 'rugby', in contrast with 'league' – and is better known around the world than Rugby League. It was strictly amateur even at the top till the mid 90s, and until the 80s was a poor relation to league in NSW and Queensland (and unfamiliar in the southern states). Its status changed with a dramatic improvement in the form of the Wallabies, the national team, who had for years been the weakest of the big eight union countries. They won the World Cup in 1991 and are still in the top four.

The two big events of the season are a state/province-level tournament between NSW, Queensland, the ACT and equivalent teams from New Zealand and South Africa, and an international series between the three southern hemisphere giants.

Professionalism is changing the game rapidly, with much higher scoring now being usual. Rugby union is played 15 a side (eight forwards); tries are worth five points, conversions two, penalty goals and field goals three. 'Unit plays' ('set' scrums, rucks, mauls and 'line-outs') are more important than in league.

SOCCER

The world game has traditionally been the poor relation of football codes in Australia, being stereotypically associated with European migrants and lacking popular support.

The main competition is now national and is played in the summer. The main catalyst for growth has again been the excellent recent form of the national team, the Socceroos and a growing interest in watching the World Cup.

THEY MAY SAY ...

sunbaking
  sunbathing

It's not really a sport but a national pastime, especially during long cricket matches and other sporting events.

CRICKET

Despite various counter-attractions, the quintessential Aussie summer sport is still cricket, transplanted from England in colonial times. Many visitors will know the game at least to some degree, but those from North America, continental Europe and most of Asia probably will not. Unfortunately, there's insufficient space here to explain cricket really adequately, and the best thing to do is probably to go to a game with a friend who can shed light on the arcane proceedings! The game is very roughly like baseball but takes up a lot more time.

Single-day matches in which each side bats once are regarded by traditionalists as travesties of 'real' cricket (two innings a side), which lasts four days at state level and five at international level – and even then often ends in a draw as neither side has time to force a win. The bowler (pitcher) must 'bowl' the ball at

DID YOU KNOW ...

The first international cricket tour of England was by a team of Aboriginal cricketers in May 1868 whose 17 members had already played at the Melbourne Cricket Ground and toured Sydney. In six months they played 47 matches against the English – victorious in 14, defeated in 14 and drawing 19. On return to Australia, the two most outstanding players – Johnny Mullagh and Jimmy Cuzens – were signed up by the Melbourne Cricket Club.

the batsman with a straight arm and must not throw it although fielders can throw it. Six balls (an 'over') are bowled at one of the two sets of stumps, which is defended by one of the two batsmen who are 'in' at any given time, and then the whole fielding side (but not the batsmen) change ends for another bowler to bowl the next over at the other set of stumps. This goes on until the innings ends, which usually takes hours (50 – 150 overs).

The aim of the bowler is to hit the stumps, to induce the batsman into hitting/edging a ball in the air and giving a catch, or to get him out in a number of other ways. The wicket-keeper behind the stumps is the prime catcher of balls edged in the air. Batsmen remain at bat until dismissed; when 10 of the 11 in the team are out, the innings is over. Each time the batsmen are able to run past each other and change ends a run is scored; if the ball crosses the boundary the batsman gets four runs (six if it doesn't bounce first). Surprising as this may seem to Americans and such, the batsmen don't have to hit fair balls bowled at them, though missing or ignoring an accurate ball may lead to dismissal by 'bowling' (the ball hits the stumps)! If the batsman does hit the ball, he doesn't have to run (another surprise!); this is a decision to be made by the two batsmen and depends on the risk of being run out and the state of the game. A good score by one batsman would be 100 and a top bowler can hope to get five of the possible 10 wickets in an innings.

Australia were runners-up in the 1996 World Cup (one-day games) played in the Indian subcontinent and are currently perhaps the best team in the world at five-day 'Test' cricket. The teams for the main domestic competitions represent the six states.

Women's Cricket

Women's cricket in Australia is not a recent sport and boasts an illustrious history on par with the Australian men's cricket teams. The first women's team was established in 1874 with a local match in Bendigo, Victoria; the first Test Match being played in Brisbane in December 1934 between teams from Australia and England. The women's team first toured England in 1937; New Zealand in 1948-49; and India in 1975.

SPORTS

The Australian women's team has won four out of six Cricket World Cups, a competition that began in 1973, two years before the introduction of the men's World Cup. Currently, the Australian Women's Cricket team is considered the best in the world in Tests (like their male counterpart) and One Day Internationals.

There are 23,000 registered female cricket players throughout Australia; not to mention the thousands more schoolgirls that are involved in their school teams but don't belong to an official cricket club.

Some Cricket Identities

David Boon	'Boonie'; favourite son of Launceston in Tasmania and a great defensive batsman for Australia
Allan Border	long-running Australian captain in the 80s and 90s, and record Test run-scorer
Sir Don Bradman	greatest batsman ever in the world, with an amazing Test career average of 99.94 in a career lasting from 1928 to 1948
Ian & Greg Chappell	brothers from a great SA cricketing family, both of whom captained Australia in the 70s
Belinda Clark	captain of the Women's Cricket team (1998). In December 1997, she became the first player (male or female) to score a double century in a One Day International.
Dennis Lillee	outstanding Test fast bowler in the 70s and early 80s
Shane Warne	the greatest leg-spin bowler of modern times, apparently headed for a world record haul of Test wickets and famous for the 'Ball from Hell' in 1993

SURF LIFESAVING

Surf lifesaving in Australia started at Manly Beach in Sydney in 1902, when a daring William Gocher broke the law by bathing in daylight. In the years that followed, 'leisure' swimming at beaches became a popular activity and drownings a common occurence. In response to these dangers of the sea, the NSW Surf Bathing Association was formed in 1907, later becoming a national body. Its members, who now number over 90,000 in some 275 clubs around the country, have performed

over 410,000 rescues, and the national championships attract large crowds. It's believed that nobody has ever drowned in Australia when swimming between the warning red and yellow flags set up by the Surf Lifesaving Association.

NETBALL

Netball was created by an American basketball coach based in England who set himself a challenge to improve the skills of basketball. After introducing this new game to several schools in England, it became a popular sport – particularly with women – and quickly spread to Australia. In recent years, the Australian teams have been very prominent players in worldwide netball competitions. Although it was established in the early days as a female sport, great interest by men led to the formation of men's and 'mixed' netball teams which are now proving very popular.

A netball court is approximately the size of a tennis court with a shooting semicircle and goal post at each end. The goalpost has no backboard and a simple hoop for shooting goals – it doesn't, as the name 'netball' may suggest, resemble the netted basket of basketball.

Each team has seven players as follows:

Goal Shooter	Wing Attack
Goal Keeper	Wing Defence
Goal Attack	Centre
Goal Defence	

Each position is restricted to a specific area on the court; only the goalshooters are able to shoot goals and only from inside the semi-circle. A player can only move two steps once they have possession of the ball and are permitted to hold the ball for only three seconds.

Indoor netball also attracts many players with rules that differ slightly to 'outdoor' netball mainly due to court size restrictions, time and the presence of nets around the court.

There are 654 netball associations in Australia, and it's estimated that 1.2 million Australians play netball including those involved in school, mixed, men's and indoor netball competitions. After being a trial sport in 1994, netball was introduced as an official sport at the 1998 Commonwealth Games – the Australian women's team winning the Gold Medal.

SPORTS

THE 2000 OLYMPICS

Along with Greece, Australia is the only country to have attended every one of the Summer Olympics. After 12 solid years of lobbying, Sydney clinched the 2000 Games by one vote ahead of first-time entrant Beijing. The first Olympics of the new millen-

HORSES, YACHTS & SURFBOARDS

Bell's Beach Surfing Classic
Each Easter weekend, Bell's Beach (southwest of Melbourne) attracts the top surfers and sunscreened spectators to the world's longest-running professional surfing competition.

Sydney to Hobart Yacht Race
For the start of this race on Boxing Day, Sydney Harbour is crammed with hundreds of seacraft from cruisers to dinghys as the competing yachts sail off toward Tasmania. There's a huge street party in Hobart to celebrate the end of this long event.

Birdsville Races
These races may not get the media coverage of the Melbourne Cup, but as Australia's premier outback race meeting, the Birdsville Races on the first weekend in September are a hugely popular event. And the beer starts flowing early ...

nium, centred at Homebush in Sydney, runs from 15 September till 1 October 2000 and involves 197 countries and 10,200 athletes competing in 28 sports.

It's the second time the sporting spectacle has been held in Australia as Melbourne played host in 1956, at the height of the Cold War. Despite some politics creeping into the competition, most notably (and bloodily) during a Hungary versus USSR men's water polo match, the Melbourne event became known as the Friendly Games.

The theme of the Sydney games is the Green Games and the Homebush site was planned to the highest environmentally friendly standards possible, including provisions for a rare species of frog living on the site. Another, more local theme, 'Share the Spirit', is aimed at convincing Australians that the games are not just a Sydney occasion.

During the Atlanta Olympics it was discovered that Australians watched on average more of the games on TV than any other country. This is an impressive statistic considering the time difference meant the telecast was mostly in the dead of night. Australia has a long list of Olympic heroes including runners Ron Clarke (who lit the Olympic flame at the 1956 opening ceremony), Herb Elliott and Betty Cuthbert; the Oarsome Foursome rowers; and swimmers Shane Gould, Kieran Perkins and the uniquely down-to-earth Dawn Fraser. More than 40% of Australia's medals have come from the swimming team, while in recent years cycling, rowing and hockey have also been strengths.

CITY & BUSH

The basic division, physically and culturally, for many Australians is the city and the bush. Most Australians live in the cities which are all, with the exception of Canberra, on the coastal fringe and because of this they tend to dream about the bush – its trees, its vast plains, its mountain ranges, its rivers and inland seas. It's achieved mythical status and is inhabited by heroes of folklore and activated by fictionalised events.

COUNTRY PLACES

There are various mythical places in this mental map of the bush.

Bullamakanka
  this is an imaginary remote town. It has a pseudo-Aboriginal name and is totally hicks-ville. It's also called Woop-Woop, or Bandy-wallop

back of Bourke
  this is a vague and unspecified area which is beyond Bourke, a remote town in north-western NSW, on the fringe of the outback. Woop-Woop and Bullamakanka are probably back of Bourke

beyond the black stump
  there are a million pubs and motels in NSW which will claim to have the authentic black stump that people went beyond – they shouldn't be believed. The phrase appears to have come from the practice of giving directions in regions where landmarks are strange-shaped rocks, hills, and the ubiquitous blackened stump. The blackened stump became the last known point of civilisation. Those who went beyond that were on their own.

the never-never
  this term refers to remote outback regions, more precisely areas of Queensland and the Northern Territory. There's a theory that the term is an anglicisation of an Aboriginal

name for the same region, Nivah Nivah, but the English version conjures up the ultimate state of being lost and forgotten.

IDENTIFIABLE REGIONS

There are regions which are identified by vegetation.

the mallee
this can apply to a number of semi-arid areas in NSW, SA and WA, but in particular to a region in Victoria where the mallee grows. The mallee is a species of eucalypt but it appears to have no trunk at all; the branches rising straight from the ground. What it does have is an enormous and tough root system, a fact that broke the hearts of many farmers who tried to dig it out. Mallee root makes good firewood as it's hard and slow-burning.

the brigalow
this is a kind of acacia or wattle. It's not an unpleasant tree but it's difficult to clear for farming because of its habit of suckering. The cattle tend to get lost in it too and will only eat the foliage when they're very hard up. One way or another it hampers operations and can cause brigalow itch, a form of dermatitis.

REVHEADS UNITE!

The Melbourne Grand Prix
Since the Formula One Grand Prix was poached from Adelaide in 1994, the inner suburban Albert Park has been completely redeveloped to host the event, much to the fury of local residents. Every March the lakeside park roars to the sound of engines and racing enthusiasts (known as revheads or petrolheads). Despite attempts by Adelaidians to lure the race back to their hometown, it seems the race will stay put for a few years yet.

CITY & BUSH

the Outback
> remote part of Australian countryside/desert

the saltbush
> sheep will eat saltbush but then it only grows in semi-desert and salty regions of central Australia where nothing else grows anyway

the scrub
> scrub is land covered by shrubby bushes, often thickly growing to the point where it's bordering on impenetrable, and indicating poor soil. To be 'out in the scrub' or 'the scrubs' is to be where no-one else particularly wants to be. It's not only remote, it's impoverished and unpleasant.

the spinifex
> spinifex is a spiny grass of a genus which is mostly found in arid zones of Australia. It's a tussocky kind of grass which puts its own stamp on the outback regions where it grows.

CITY & BUSH

EUROPEANS & THE BUSH

The bush of Australians' collective memory has the whitening bones of explorers, the cries of 'Bail up!' from the bushrangers, the farmers ranging from the cocky farmers to the bunyip aristocracy, the bushmen and the swaggies.

The Explorers

In the Australian way, the European explorers who live on in popular imagination are not the plodding and orthodox types like Sir Thomas Mitchell, a worthy surveyor and Government man who did a lot of good work in New South Wales and Victoria. The people Australians remember are the glorious failures, such as Burke and Wills, the pair who set out from Victoria to cross the continent in 1860. Robert O'Hara Burke was a dashing character whose impetuous decision to lead an expedition through the desert led to the death of the entire group. Another example is Ludwig Leichhardt, a German who arrived in Sydney in 1842 and was considered somewhat eccentric by conservative

Sydney (Sir Thomas Mitchell didn't take to him at all). But after one successful and one dismal expedition, he set out into the Outback with a small party and was never seen again. This foray inspired Patrick White's novel *Voss*.

The Bushrangers

Bushranging begins and ends with Ned (Edward) Kelly (1855–80) who led the troopers a merry dance until he was finally caught and hanged in Melbourne Gaol. There are a lot of elements in the story which have led to Ned becoming a kind of Robin Hood figure in Australian folklore, but the story of his capture is unique. Ned and his gang (mostly his brothers) had held up the entire town of Glenrowan in Victoria. Meanwhile the Melbourne establishment had sent out a train of police and trackers. Ned organised fettlers (railway workers) to dig up the tracks and derail the train, but the Glenrowan schoolmaster escaped and managed to stop the train in time. The bushrangers realised their plan had failed and donned home-made armour made from the metal of ploughs for the final shoot-out. But despite the armour the bushrangers were outnumbered. Ned's last words before he was hanged were said to be 'Such is life!'

There are a couple of other bushrangers who are worth a mention. Captain Moonlight and Captain Thunderbolt were good bushmen and rather elegant performers. Brave Ben Hall was in the more sinned against than in the sinning category – he took to bushranging because of basic injustice. Mad Dog Morgan on the other hand was noted for his brutality.

The Farmers

These fall into different categories:

cocky farmer
>   a cocky is a small landholder – the idea is that this kind of farmer resembles the cockatoo who scratches in the dirt to find a living. A cocky can be a cane cocky (sugar farmer), a cow cocky (dairy farmer) or a wheat cocky (wheat farmer).

grazier

a grazier is a station-owner and runs sheep or cattle. The grazier is the big landowner and much more likely to be part of the bunyip aristocracy or squattocracy, the *crème de la crème* of the bush.

jackeroo

a jackeroo was a young man sent out to gain experience on a station, usually as a preliminary to running one of his own. The word is borrowed from an Aboriginal word, taken to mean 'wandering white man'. After the jackeroo came the jillaroo – the female counterpart.

MORE BUSH TERMS

backblocks	a remote area
blaze	to cut bark from a tree; acts as a reference point marking in the bush
bushcraft	ability to survive on your own in the bush with limited equipment
bushbash	to force your way through untouched bushland
bush telegraph	town gossip grapevine
bush telly	watching the stars
cleanskin	unbranded cattle
dover	bush knife
duffing	stealing cattle
droving	moving cattle or sheep (see overlander)
humpy	bush dwelling using cheap materials
overlander	a stockman on horseback that drives livestock over long distances
poddy dodger	cattle rustler
'roo/bull bar	bumper bar on the front of a vehicle
tuckerbag	a bag for carrying and storing food
woof wood	petrol used to get a fire going

The Shearers

shearer
sheep-shearers are celebrated in the song 'Click Go the Shears Boys'

The ringer looks around and is beaten by a blow,
And curses the old swaggie with the bare-belly yeo.

Shearing has its own jargon — masses of it. The ringer is the fastest shearer in the shed, the one who runs rings around everyone else, but in this instance he's beaten by one blow, that is, one stroke of the shears. And what's worse he's beaten by an old swaggie, a nobody in the shearer's world. The reason the swaggie won is that he has a bare-belly yeo or ewe, a sheep that has defective wool growth that makes the wool come off easily.

rouseabout
a rouseabout is a station hand who's expected to do all the odd jobs. In the shearing shed he's the one who rushes up with the tar for a cut sheep and who gathers up the fleeces and takes them to the sorting table.

More Country People

boundary rider
while every station has fences which can cover vast acreage and which need to be regularly maintained, there have been incredibly long fences erected by State Governments for various reasons: to keep rabbits from crossing from eastern Australia to Western Australia or to keep dingoes out of settled NSW. Boundary riders patrolled these fences, often not seeing another human being for months on end.

DID YOU KNOW ... The champion shearer in each shearing shed is called the gun shearer

There's a tradition of boundary riders who are loners by nature and self-educated men, happy to be by themselves in the bush and armed with the complete works of Shakespeare in their saddlebag.

bushie
the bushman or bushie is the man who lives in the bush. The idea of the bushman is that he's totally at home in it and knows all its ways, he's never lost and

PITT STREET FARMER

LE WEEKEN

never starves or dies of thirst, and he's usually on good terms with the Aborigines from whom he's learnt a thing or two.

swagman

the swagman or swaggie is the man who carries his swag on the wallaby track (shortened to 'on the wallaby'). Often a good bushman too. The sundowner is the swaggie who times his arrival at a station (sheep or cattle station) at about sundown, too late to be asked to do any work in return for his tea and sugar and flour.

THE CITY

The city is referred to by bushies as the big smoke and its inhabitants are city slickers. City people are considered fast and dishonest and the bushies only way of handling them is to be bold and upstanding.

The city/bush division still lives on in the country, but Australian cities have changed a lot in the last decade or so and are rather less concerned with the country and more concerned with either themselves – there's a lot of city introspection – or with the outside world, particularly the USA.

City Terms

city

this is an important and confusing term in Australian English with various meanings. 'The city' refers to either the whole of Sydney, for example, or to just the central part of it. There's a basic distinction between a city which is very big and a town which can be big or small but which is less important than a city. In the country 'the city' can either be the city or the whole area surrounding it. You can be driving through the middle of nowhere and find a sign which states that you're now in the City of Bullamakanka. But you may have to drive for a while before you actually find any real signs of civilisation, as city status is conferred by regional population numbers not on the size of the metropolis.

inner city
>anywhere within walking distance of the main post office

inner suburbs
>this is the ring of suburbs just beyond the inner city, that is, about seven kilometres from the GPO. In Sydney the concept of the inner city is complicated by such facts as that most people don't consider

GO TO TOWN ...
Sometimes you'll hear people from the suburbs say they're **'going to town'** for the day when they mean going to the city centre. They could live ten minutes away but they'll still say this.

North Sydney, for example, to be inner city. Once across the bridge (or through the tunnel) you're on the North Shore, which is a world unto itself. The inner city is a trendy place to live – café societies, etc.

outer suburbs
>beyond the ring of the inner city are the outer suburbs, essentially hicksville. In Sydney westies live in the outer suburbs and are considered by inner city folk to be uncool, dorks, nerds, bevans, bogans, etc. They are, in lifestyle, the antithesis of both the surfies who live on the beaches and the rad city dudes.

the suburbs
>'the suburbs', or the 'burbs, have been an object of derision boring, dreary, etc, but are beginning to be discovered as having a life of their own.

Housing Terms

apartment
>this term isn't so common but refers to an up-market flat. A studio apartment is a small one-room flat.

brick veneer
>these are timber-framed homes with exteriors of brick in

different shades – red or beige or brown with flecks of black   – and roofs of terracotta. This style of house dominates the 'burb-scape.

bungalow
the Californian bungalow is one of the basic housing styles of the Australian suburb. This basic architectural style imported from the goldfields of California in the 1850s has been adapted to Australian conditions perhaps more satisfactorily than any other. It's typically one storey with a buttress-like stone or pebble chimney, a deep verandah, and a simple, low-pitched spreading gabled tiled roof.

cluster house
this is one of a group of houses which share a block of land, a space-saver in suburbia where urban consolidation is the catchcry

condo
this is a condominium or large apartment. They tend to have sale prices of over a million

duplex
this can be a two-storey block of flats or home units, each dwelling occupying one floor

façadism
this practice involves retaining the façade of an old building while constructing a new one behind it

Federation Style
characterised by a red brick exterior, terracotta roof tiles and chimney pots, and heavy window frames, houses built in this style of architecture date back to between 1890 and 1920

flat
this is the basic term for a living space generally in an apartment building or divided house

granny flat
during the days of the Depression, this was called a sleep-out, and is now quaintly called a chalet in Tasmania. It's a

small building out the back which can be used as a separate dwelling.

home unit

this is a division of a housing block which has a number of such dwellings in it; the term may be shortened to unit

queenslander

exclusive to Queensland (and Darwin, before Cyclone Tracy blew them all down in 1974), these timber homes have wide open verandahs and are elevated on stilts to make the most of the cool breezes

semi-detached

this is one of a pair of houses joined by a common wall

CITY & BUSH

DID YOU KNOW ...

A booming business in Queensland is the transplanting of queenslander houses from the original block to another, in a neighbouring suburb or a faraway town. As if in a supermarket, buyers meander through rows of these charming timber houses propped up on bricks and choose their dream home. For a fee, the house is sliced in two, lifted onto wide trucks, driven – slowly – to the empty block during the night (for obvious reasons) and 're-built'. Voila!

terrace house
Paddington terrace houses in Sydney are famous for the charm of the wrought iron on their balconies and the wealth of their owners. However, terrace houses are common enough. They were basically last century's cheap housing for the poor, but since WWII have become trendy housing for inner city dwellers.

villa
this is a classier kind of modern terrace, slightly bigger and with better bathrooms and kitchens

weatherboard
a house made of timber

Australia's States & Territories

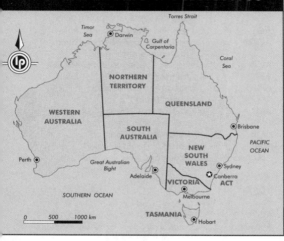

STATES & TERRITORIES

Australia consists of six states and two territories.

New South Wales	NSW
Queensland	Qld
South Australia	SA
Tasmania	Tas
Victoria	Vic
Western Australia	WA
Australian Capital Territory	ACT
Northern Territory	NT

ACRONYMS & ABBREVIATIONS

7-Eleven	convenience store
AAP	*Australian Associated Press*
AAT	*Australian Antarctic Territory*
ABC	*Australian Broadcasting Corporation* (nicknamed 'Auntie')
AC	*Companion of the Order of Australia*
ACTU	*Australian Council of Trade Unions* (pronounce each letter)
ACF	*Australian Conservation Foundation*
AFI	*Australian Film Institute*
AFL	*Australian Football League*
ALP	*Australian Labor Party*
AM	*Member of the Order of Australia*
AMA	*Australian Medical Association*
AMF	*Australian Military Forces*
ANU	*Australian National University* (Canberra)
ANZAAS	*Australian and New Zealand Association for the Advancement of Science* (pronounced an-zas)
ANZAC	*Australian and New Zealand Army Corps* (pronounced an-zak)
AO	*Officer of the Order of Australia*
ASEAN	*Association of South-East Asian Nations* (pronounced ay-zee-an)
ASIO	*Australian Security Intelligence Organisation* (pronounced ay-zee-oh)
ASIS	*Australian Secret Intelligence Service*
ASX	*Australian Stock Exchange*
ATC	*Australian Tourist Commission*
ATO	*Australian Taxation Office*
BASS	ticket office for major entertainment events (rhymes with 'gas')
BCA	*Business Council of Australia*
BYO(G)	*Bring your own (grog).* Some restaurants are only licensed for patrons to bring wine, etc with them.

CAA	*Community Aid Abroad (Australian Oxfam)*
CHOGM	*Commonwealth Heads of Government Meeting (pronounced chog-um)*
COAG	*Council of Australian Governments (pronounced ko-ag)*
C of E	*Church of England*
CPI	*Consumer Price Index*
CSIRO	*Commonwealth Scientific & Industrial Research Organisation*
CST	*Central Standard Time (South Australia & the Northern Territory – 9.5 hours ahead of GMT/UTC)*
CWA	*Country Women's Association*
DLP	*Democratic Labor Party*
EG	*The Entertainment Guide in Friday's The Age (Melbourne newspaper). This is the one to read for info on what to do, see and listen to.*
EPA	*Environment Protection Authority*
EST	*Eastern Standard Time (10 hours ahead of Greenwich Mean Time. All eastern states are in this zone.)*
GG	*Governor-General*
GPO	*General Post Office*
GST	*Goods & Services Tax*
HMAS	*Her Majesty's Australian Ship*
HR	*House of Representatives*
HSC	*Higher School Certificate*
LA	*Legislative Assembly*
M	*Films, TV for mature audiences (15 years and over)*
MCG	*Melbourne Cricket Ground*
MHA	*Member of the House of Assembly*
MHR	*Member of the House of Representatives*
MLA	*Member of the Legislative Assembly*
MLC	*Member of the Legislative Council*
MLG	*Member of Local Government*

MP	*Member of Parliament*
MTC	*Melbourne Theatre Company*. The principal theatre company in Melbourne.
NGA	*National Gallery of Australia*
NGV	*National Gallery of Victoria*
NIDA	*National Institute of Dramatic Art* (pronounced *nigh-dah*)
NRMA	*National Roads & Motorists' Association* (of New South Wales)
OAM	*Medal of the Order of Australia*
OM	*Order of Merit*
OYO	*own your own apartment*
PAYE	*Pay as you earn*
PG	(Films, TV) parental guidance (recommended for children under 15)
PIN	*Personal Identification Number*
R	(Films, TV) unsuitable for people under the age of 18 years of age; stands for 'restricted exhibition'
RAAF	*Royal Australian Air Force*
RACV	*Royal Automobile Club of Victoria*. The equivalent of the AA in the UK and New Zealand.
RACQ	*Royal Automobile Club of Queensland*
RAN	*Royal Australian Navy*
RBA	*Reserve Bank of Australia*
RMIT	*Royal Melbourne Institute of Technology*
RRP	*Recommended Retail Price*
RSL	*Returned Services League* (of Australia)
RSPCA	*Royal Society for the Prevention of Cruelty to Animals*
RWC	*Road Worthy Certificate*. Obligatory safety check before a car changes hands (Victoria)
SCG	*Sydney Cricket Ground*
SM	*Stipendiary Magistrate*
SBS	*Special Broadcasting Service*. TV and radio station focusing on multicultural programmes.

STA	*State Transit Authority* (NSW).
STC	*Sydney Theatre Company*
STD	*Subscriber Trunk Dialling*. You need to use STD codes when dialling numbers outside local zones.
TAFE	*Technical & Further Education* (pronounced *tayf*)
TEC	*Tertiary Education Commission*
TPC	*Trade Practices Commission*
VAT	*value added tax* (vat)
VFA	*Victorian Football Association*
V/Line	interstate and country train services in Victoria
WEA	*Workers' Educational Association*
WRAAF	*Women's Royal Australian Air Force*
WRAN	*Women's Royal Association Navy*
WST	*Western Standard Time* (Western Australia – eight hours ahead of Greenwich Meantime)
YHA	*Youth Hostels Association* (now known world wide as Hostelling International)
YMCA	*Young Men's Christian Association*
YWCA	*Young Women's Christian Association*

AUSTRALIAN
ABORIGINAL
LANGUAGES

INTRODUCTION

The original inhabitants of Australia have been living on this continent for tens of thousands of years. When the British established the first European settlement in Australia at Port Jackson (Sydney) in 1788, the newcomers originally called the older inhabitants 'natives' and then 'Aborigines'. The latter term is in general use, but some Aboriginal people prefer one of their own names rather than 'Aborigine', which can be applied to any indigenous people. There's no self-designation that covers all Aboriginal people; the term Murri is used in Queensland, Nyungar or Nyoongah in the south-west of Western Australia, Yolŋu in north-eastern Arnhem Land and Koori or Koorie in New South Wales and Victoria.

The size of the Aboriginal population at the time the first Europeans came to Australia is not known, but estimates run from a low of 300,000 to over a million. The people were hunter-gatherers, that is they lived by hunting animals and gathering various plant foods. Each person belonged to a land-owning group, typically a clan with its own distinctive speech. Often a group of neighbouring clans would have similar forms of speech and we could say that these clans spoke dialects of a particular language. It's now extremely difficult to ascertain the number of languages spoken prior to contact with Europeans, especially in areas where the Aboriginal population was wiped out and records of languages spoken are few. But it's clear that there were a great number of languages spoken throughout the land. It's estimated that in 1788 there were about 250 different languages in Australia, each comprising several dialects. However, over the course of the next 100 years the British took over the whole of Australia and in the process many Aboriginal people died, either as a result of introduced diseases or through being shot or poisoned. In areas where fertile land attracted a denser pattern of European settlement, most of the Aboriginal population perished.

Today there are no speakers left of the languages of Tasmania, Victoria, and most of New South Wales. The only flourishing languages are to be found in the centre of the continent and along the north coast.

RELATEDNESS

There is no clear connection between the languages of the mainland or those of Tasmania. Nor, indeed, is there a known connection between the languages of the mainland and Tasmania and any languages spoken elsewhere.

On the mainland, one way of classifying the languages is by distinguishing between Pama-Nyungan and non-Pama-Nyungan language families. Pama-Nyungan is a very large group both in terms of numbers and the area the languages cover. The word Pama-Nyungan was made up out of the name for 'man, person' from the most north-easterly representative and the most south-westerly representative of this large language family. The Pama-Nyungan languages were spoken over the majority of the mainland and have a percentage of shared vocabulary, language structure and sounds that indicates a possible shared predecessor language. However, Pama and Nyunga vary widely and there are few outstanding similarities between these languages, just as there are few overt similarities between such related languages as English, Russian and Hindi.

The languages known as the non-Pama-Nyungan group are located to the north (the Top End) and the north-west (Kimberleys) of the mainland. The relationships between the various languages of this group are as yet unclear.

SOUNDS

There is some similarity among the Aboriginal languages with some of the sounds they use and the way these sounds are strung together. All the languages have the ng sound as in 'sing' and it's common for this sound to appear at the beginning of a word.

The word for 'I', for instance, is often ngaya or something similar. Another common sound is ny as in bunya, the Yagara name of a tall pine-like tree found in south-eastern Queensland. This sound may also occur at the beginning of a word, as in Nyungar, the name of the language and people of south-western Western Australia. There are also 'r-coloured' sounds such as rn in murnong, the yam daisy of Victoria, and rd as in nardoo, a kind of flour made from the spores of various ferns. This word is actually ngardu and comes from the languages of western New South Wales and neighbouring states. These 'r-coloured' sounds are much the same as in the middle of words like 'mourner' and 'warder' in a typical American pronunciation. Certain sounds found in English don't occur, such as s, z and sh and the sounds f, v and h.

In Aboriginal languages there's normally no distinction between members of the following pairs: p/b, t/d, k/g, and ch (also spelled ty or tj) and j (also spelled dy or dj). This is part of the reason that the names of some groups and their languages are variously spelled, such as Arunta/Aranda, nowadays Arrernte (central Australia), and Walbiri/Warlpiri (central Australia). Alternation between the members of these pairs can be a problem when it comes to using reference books, particularly where the alternation is in the initial consonant. The name of the original inhabitants of the Adelaide area, for instance, is spelled both Kaurna and Gaurna.

Some Australian Languages have dental sounds. These are written th (or dh), nh and lh. Sometimes an underline is used, but it should be noted that an underline is also used in some areas for 'r-coloured' sounds (see above). A dental t sounds a little like th in English, but dental n and dental l are so similar to ordinary n and l in English that they can be distinguished only with practice. Another distinctive feature is the 'y-coloured' sounds made by holding the tip of the tongue down behind the lower front teeth while making such sounds as t, n and l. These sounds are often written with a y, as in ty, ny and ly.

Since Aboriginal words often contain sounds and sound sequences unfamiliar to speakers of English, they've often been recorded with various degrees of accuracy. The inaccurate rendering of ngardu was mentioned above. This word is also found as ardu with the initial ng missing altogether.

There are also problems with conveying the sounds of Aboriginal words accurately because of the irregular relationship between sound and spelling in English. For instance, in English the letter 'u' represents one sound in 'but' and another in 'put'. The language of the bayside areas around Melbourne was recorded as Bunwurung and Bunarong, which gives a poor guide to the pronunciation. It's also recorded as Boonoorong which gives a better guide to the pronunciation of the vowels, but Bunarong has been perpetuated as the name of a park and several streets, and is pronounced in a way that the bearers of that name would never recognise.

Typical Aboriginal words have more than one syllable. They usually begin with a consonant and end with a vowel, and they don't normally contain awkward sequences of consonants that are hard to pronounce. The following words borrowed from Aboriginal languages are fairly typical:

barramundi	type of fish, especially Lates Calcarifer (central Queensland coast)
boobialla	shrubs of the Myoporum genus (south-eastern Tasmania)
corroboree	ceremony with singing and dancing (Dharuk, Sydney area)
wallaby	kangaroo-like animal (Dharuk, Sydney area)

However, in most Aboriginal languages the main stress is on the first syllable. Of the words quoted above only wallaby maintains what was probably the original stress.

VOCABULARY

It has been a mistaken belief that Aboriginal languages have only a few words. In fact, like any language they have thousands. Many of these words don't correspond directly to English words, rather they cover a different classification of the natural world and express concepts particular to Aboriginal culture.

A striking feature of Aboriginal vocabulary is that the words found in one language are usually quite different from those found in neighbouring languages and elsewhere. This means that if you learn one Aboriginal language, you don't have much of a start for learning a second one. However, there are a few words that are widespread. This core of words includes the following:

bina	ear	jina	foot
bula	two	mara	hand
jalayn	tongue	mili	eye
jarra	thigh		

STRUCTURE

Aboriginal languages characteristically use different endings, added to words, to mark relations between words in a sentence. In the Kalkadoon language of the Mount Isa area, for instance, an ending is used to mark a word denoting the entity responsible for an action. In the following example the ending -yu is attached to the word martu, 'mother'.

Mother grabs the dog.   Martu-yu ngulurmayi thuku.

Since the suffix -yu indicates that it's the mother who grabs the dog rather than the dog who grabs the mother, the word order can be varied to show different degrees of emphasis. You could have the following, for instance.

Mother grabs the dog.   Ngulurmayi thuku martu-yu.

Here are two more endings: -piangu meaning 'from' and -kunha meaning 'to'.

The policeman goes   Kanimayintyirr ingka
   from Darwin to   Darwin-piangu Melbourne-
   Melbourne.   kunha

The word kanimayintyirr means 'policeman'. Literally it's 'the one who ties up'; kanimayi is 'tie up' and -nytyirr is a suffix like '-er' in English words such as 'driver'. This is an interesting example of how the Kalkadoon people made up a new word for the new concept of policeman.

Across the north of the continent languages tend to have very complex verbs that seem more like sentences than single words. In Tiwi, the language of Bathurst and Melville Islands, for instance, the English sentence 'He sent them a message' can be expressed as a single word yu-wuni-marri-wa-yangirri, literally, 'he-them-with-words-sent'.

DEVELOPMENTS

As in other parts of the world where European colonisation and accompanying social disruption has taken place, creole languages have arisen in northern Australia. Two widespread creoles, Broken and Kriol, are spoken by many Aboriginal people in the Torres Strait and in the Top End respectively.

The sound system and certain areas of vocabulary are heavily influenced by the traditional languages of the region. Although the vocabulary of both Broken and Kriol is largely of English origin, many of these words have changed in meaning to embody traditional concepts and distinctions. In English the word 'we' refers to the speaker and one or more other persons. Aboriginal languages usually have a number of words for 'we', distinguishing whether 'we' covers two people or more than two, and whether the addressee (you) is included. These distinctions are carried over into the creoles. In the Kriol of Roper River, for instance, yunmi means 'we' in the sense of 'you and I', mintupala means 'we two' (not including you) and there are a number of words for 'we' covering more than two people. These include wi, melapat and mipala.

Well over a hundred of the original 250 or so languages have died and only a few will survive into the next century, including several varieties of Kriol. However, Aboriginal people all over Australia are showing a renewed interest in preserving what they can of their languages and in trying to restore them from materials recorded during past generations. In many parts of Australia the present generation of Aboriginal children is being taught the language that belongs to their particular area.

CENTRAL AUSTRALIAN LANGUAGES

The languages in central Australia – or the Centre, as it's often referred to – are among the strongest surviving Aboriginal languages in the country, as their speakers have had a relatively short history of contact with non-Aboriginal people. Despite this, the effects of non-Aboriginal settlement have been dramatic. Before non-Aboriginal people began to settle in central Australia in the 1870s, it's thought that there were at least 38 main languages and dialects in the area. The establishment of pastoral properties, the Overland Telegraph Line, missions and reserves and later towns such as Alice Springs has had a huge impact on the original inhabitants of central Australia. It's meant that many language groups have moved, or have been moved, from their traditional country, resulting in language change and, in some cases, language loss to the point of extinction. Of the original 38 main languages and dialects, about seven are now considered endangered, and four are considered extinct or nearly extinct.

The main surviving language groups in central Australia are the group of Arandic languages and dialects, dialects of the Western Desert language, dialects of Warlpiri and Warumungu. These languages belong to the Pama-Nyungan family of languages (see page 150). Unlike the fertile land in the Top End of Australia, or along the east coast of the continent, the arid lands of central Australia can only support a limited number of people. As a result, single language groups are spread over vast areas of land. The Western Desert language for example is one of the most widely spread indigenous languages in the world, extending from central Australia to the Great Australian Bight and the Indian Ocean.

Many language speakers are bilingual or multilingual, speaking one or more Aboriginal languages or dialects as well as English. Although languages in the Centre share a few common characteristics, they are for the most part very different from each other. The names of languages and dialects used in central Australia

CENTRAL AUSTRALIA

have become quite widely known. Often, they describe where the people who speak that language come from, or describe a feature of their language which distinguishes it from another language nearby:

Ikngerre-ipenhe Arrernte	eastern Arrernte
Pitjantjatjara	having the word pitja ('come')

KEEPING LANGUAGES STRONG

Apart from speaking their languages to their children and grand-children, Aboriginal people are working hard in language centres, schools and media outlets to ensure that their languages survive. In Alice Springs, the Central Australian Aboriginal Media Association (CAAMA) broadcasts programs in English and in local languages. Also in Alice Springs, Imparja Television broadcasts occasional programs in Aboriginal languages with English subtitles (for example, Nganampa Anwernekenhe – check local papers for program details).

There are a number of bands playing contemporary and more traditional Aboriginal music, including songs in Aboriginal languages, around the Centre. The CAAMA Shops (see details below under Further Reading on page 164) stock cassette tapes, compact discs and some videos of local Aboriginal bands.

In Alice Springs, the Language and Culture Centre at the Institute for Aboriginal Development (IAD, PO Box 2531, Alice Springs, 0871) runs language and cross-culture programs for Aboriginal and non-Aboriginal people from Alice Springs, as well as interstate and international visitors. The Institute also carries out research into central Australian languages, and produces dictionaries and other language-related publications. In Tennant Creek, Papulu Apparr-kari (the Barkly Region Aboriginal Language Centre, PO Box 1108, Tennant Creek, 0861) coordinates language and culture programs for the Barkly region.

There are several bilingual schools in the central Australian region, where Aboriginal children learn in both their own language and in English. Most of these schools are in Aboriginal communities, apart from Yipirinya School, an independent school in Alice Springs. Aboriginal people can study their own languages, or prepare for careers in interpreting and translating, language teaching or dictionary work by attending courses run by the IAD or Batchelor College, an Aboriginal college based at Batchelor (south of Darwin) that has campuses in both Alice Springs and Tennant Creek.

TALKING WITH ABORIGINAL PEOPLE

Some Aboriginal people in central Australia speak standard Australian English. Others, especially those who speak another language as their first language, may use a different kind of English, often known as Aboriginal English. Aboriginal English uses mostly English words, but takes its grammar, sounds and most of its cultural meanings from Aboriginal languages.

Many travellers would be aware of how insulting it is to be spoken to in 'pidgin' by a fluent speaker of a language. Or of how frustrating it is when someone speaks to you in a loud voice – as if you were deaf, rather than unable to understand the language. It's important to remember this when speaking to people who don't speak English as their first language. Speak slowly and clearly, but don't insult people by using baby talk or a kind of pidgin language, and don't speak in a voice that's louder than your normal speaking voice.

Asking direct questions (especially 'why' questions such as 'Why aren't you coming?') is considered rude by many Aboriginal people. It's better to make suggestions or to talk around the issue, than to ask direct questions. Don't always expect exact replies to your questions either. It's unlikely that you'll be given anything but the most public information by people that you've just met. Don't embarrass people by asking questions about anything that could be considered private, or expect that people have got the time to stop and answer all of your questions. Many Aboriginal people are tired of being harassed by non-Aboriginal people on a search for spiritual or cultural knowledge, but may be too polite to say so. If you're particularly interested in finding out more about Aboriginal culture, you may want to join a tour organised by Aboriginal people (see page 163), or enrol in a language or cross-culture course organised by the Institute for Aboriginal Development or Papulu Apparr-kari.

Central Australian languages, like most Australian languages don't have words for greetings like 'hello'. Aboriginal people are now accustomed to English speakers using greetings, and some languages have adopted greetings based on the English form. These are used mainly to greet non-Aboriginal people, especially those who have begun to learn the language. Language speakers don't use these greetings when talking to each other. Instead, they often call out a person's 'skin' name or use a relationship term (see page 162).

Likewise, central Australian languages don't have words for 'please' or 'thank you'. Although these days, more and more people use the English 'thank you', thanks is expressed in actions

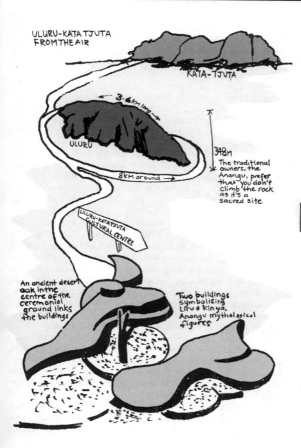

ULURU-KATA TJUTA
FROM THE AIR

KATA-TJUTA

← 3·6 KM long →

ULURU

348m
The traditional
owners, the
Anangu, prefer
that you don't
climb the rock
as it's a
sacred site

8 KM around →

ULURU-KATATJUTA
CULTURAL CENTRE

An ancient desert
oak in the
centre of the
ceremonial
ground links
the buildings

Two buildings
symbolising
Liru & kinya,
Anangu mythological
figures

rather than words. If someone does something for you, you show your thanks by doing something for that person or a relative at a later date. Similarly, if someone gives you something, it would be appropriate to reciprocate by giving them or a relative something in return at another time. Money may be given, or material goods, knowledge, or even friendship in exchange.

It's not polite to ask people 'What's your name?', as many English speakers may do to start a conversation. If you want to know a person's name, it's better to ask another person nearby 'What's that person's name?'. A better way of starting a conversation is to refer to a recent local event, or perhaps to admire a child who's with the person you're speaking with. The best way is to tell them where you're from, and ask them where they're from. Among Aboriginal language speaking adults, first names are used much less than in non-Aboriginal society. People tend to use relationship terms, such as 'uncle' or 'daughter' when talking to each other. Members of some language groups, notably Warlpiri, refer to each other by 'skin' names.

Many Aboriginal people use hand signs and gestures during everyday conversation and during ceremonies. These signs are not limited to the deaf community, but are used and understood by all language speakers. As you walk around Alice Springs, you may be aware of people using handsigns to communicate with each other across long distances, like across the Todd River or busy roads, or in other situations where talking or shouting is not practical.

Aboriginal people don't use eye contact as much as non-Aboriginal people. There are times when eye contact is extremely inappropriate, for example, in certain kin relationships or between men and women who don't know each other. As a woman you may find it very refreshing to be able to walk past a large group of men without even a glance, let alone a whistle! It's very important not to embarrass people by staring. Remember that you may end up embarrassing yourself if your stares are interpreted as indicating sexual interest.

It isn't polite to talk to a mother-to-be or a father-to-be about the child they're going to have. Aboriginal women may talk among themselves about pregnancy, but questions or interest from a stranger about this topic is likely to embarrass people into an awkward silence.

It's both offensive and upsetting for many Aboriginal people in central Australia to hear the name of a close relative or friend who has recently passed away. The deceased should not be referred to directly, but rather a close relative is described as bereaved (of a son, daughter, etc). If someone has the same name, or a name that sounds the same as a person who's just passed away, then they may be given a new name, or they may be referred to as kwementyaye (Arrernte), kumanjayi (Warlpiri) or kunmanara (Pitjantjatjara). It's also offensive to show photographs of a person who's recently passed away.

FAMILY RELATIONSHIPS

Aboriginal people in central Australia think of themselves as related to all the people in their own language group, and often to people in other language groups as well. To regulate social behaviour, law and ceremony, and relationship to land, Aboriginal societies are typically divided up into two or three sets of 'moieties' (essentially a moiety is a division of the society into two opposed and balanced halves). In many parts of northern Australia, the kinship and moiety groupings have been summarised in a neat and efficient way through what are commonly known as 'skin' groups or sub-sections. The most common pattern is for there to be eight 'skin' groups, often further divided into male and female groups (see the following chart). A person is born into one of these 'skin' groups and acquires the name of that 'skin' group as well as a personal name. Various relatives are classed together in each 'skin' group. A person's position within this system determines their relationship and social and ceremonial obligations to all others in the language group. Kinship systems are too complex to describe fully here. There are several books available that give an overview of kinship in central Australia, including *A Simple Introduction to Central Australian Kinship Systems* by Jim Wafer (IAD publications, 1982).

CENTRAL AUSTRALIA

CENTRAL AUSTRALIAN ABORIGINAL 'SKIN' NAMES

LANGUAGE GROUPS		WESTERN DESERT NGAANYATJARRA	PINTUPI/ LURITJA	WARLPIRI	ARRERNTE & ANMATYERR
SUB-SECTION	*male*	Yiparrka	Tjangala	Jangala	Angale
	female		Nangala	Nangala	
SECTION					
SUB-SECTION	*male*	Panaka	Tjupurrula	Jupurrurla	Perrurle
	female		Napurrula	Napurrurla	
MOIETY	'Sun-side'				
SUB-SECTION	*male*		Tjungurrayi	Jungarrayi	Kngwarraye
	female		Nungurrayi	Nungurrayi	
SECTION		Tjarurru			
SUB-SECTION	*male*		Tjapanangka	Japanangka	Penangke
	female		Njapanangka	Njapanangka	
SUB-SECTION	*male*	Milangka	Tjampitjinpa	Jampijinpa	Ampetyane
	female		Nampitjinpa	Nampijinpa	
SECTION					
SUB-SECTION	*male*	Karimarra	Tjakamarra	Jakamarra	Kemarre
	female		Nakamarra	Nakamarra	
MOIETY	'Shade-side'				
SUB-SECTION	*male*		Tjapangati	Japangardi	Pengarte
	female		Napangati	Napangardi	
SECTION		Purungu			
SUB-SECTION	*male*		Tjapaltjarri	Japaljarri	Peltharre
	female		Napaltjarri	Napaljarri	

TRAVELLING & STAYING ON ABORIGINAL LAND

Apart from major town centres like Alice Springs and Tennant Creek, many Aboriginal people in central Australia live in remote communities and out-stations, many of which are on Aboriginal land. Most Aboriginal communities don't welcome visitors, except those people who have a genuine reason to visit (for example, people who are connected with Aboriginal organisations or government departments, or who have been invited by someone in the community).

Some communities have established tourism ventures, such as Wallace Rockhole, and Hermannsburg south-west of Alice Springs. For information about tour operators in the southern half of the Northern Territory, contact the Central Land Council (PO Box 3321, Alice Springs, 0871). For information about tour operators on the Anangu Pitjantjatjara Lands in the northern part of South Australia, contact: Anangu Pitjantjatjara (PMB Umuwa, via Alice Springs 0872); Desert Tracks (PO Box 360, Yulara, 0872); or the Aboriginal Art and Culture Centre (86 Todd St, Alice Springs 0871 (tel (08)89523408, http://www.aboriginalart.com.au)

You'll need a permit to visit or travel through all communities on Aboriginal land in central Australia, and as this can sometimes take a few weeks to process, it's better to plan ahead. (Contact the Central Land Council's Permit Office.)

If you're fortunate enough to have the opportunity to visit an Aboriginal community, don't leave the community on your own to go for a walk or do a bit of sightseeing. Ask an Aboriginal person to go with you. They'll make sure that you don't stumble across any ceremonial camps or sacred areas that you shouldn't see. Also, make an effort to dress appropriately – make sure that your clothes are clean, and avoid revealing or tight clothing.

CENTRAL AUSTRALIA

TAKING PHOTOGRAPHS

It's important to observe the usual courtesies in taking photographs of people – make sure that you ask for permission first, and if practical, offer to send copies of the photographs to your subjects. It's also extremely important not to photograph sacred sites. In some popular tourist destinations, such as Uluru, there are signs at sacred sites requesting that you don't take photographs or use a video camera. Commercial photography and filming is prohibited in many areas. Contact the Central Land Council or Anangu Pitjantjatjara for details.

You are not allowed to carry alcohol into most central Australian Aboriginal communities. This rule is strictly enforced. If you're found carrying alcohol into a dry community your vehicle will be taken from you as penalty. Most vehicles aren't returned, so it's very foolish to take this risk. Where this rule is in place, it applies to all people living in the community, both Aboriginal and non-Aboriginal.

FURTHER READING

There are several places in Alice Springs that stock a range of books about Aboriginal culture and languages, and some that also sell paintings and artefacts. A few of these are owned by Aboriginal groups. These include: IAD Press and the Aboriginal Art and Culture Centre or contact CAAMA Shops Pty Ltd (wholesale), 101 Todd St, Alice Springs (tel (08) 8952 9207). IAD Press is the publishing arm of the Institute For Aboriginal Development which publishes materials produced by and for Aboriginal people, about the languages and cultures of Central Australia. Contact IAD Press for an up-to-date catalogue. IAD Press, Institute for Aboriginal Development, PO Box 2531, Alice Springs, NT 0871 (tel (08) 8951 1334, fax (08) 8952 2527 email <iadpress@peg.apc.org>). All the books mentioned in this chapter are available from these outlets.

ARRERNTE
Languages & Dialects

The language name spelt Arrernte in the spelling system used for writing in this language, is perhaps better known outside central Australia as Aranda or Arunta. This language is part of a group of closely related languages and dialects known to linguists as the Arandic group (see map, page 166). The major language in this group has a number of dialects, including Central, Eastern, Western and Southern Arrernte, Eastern and Western Anmatyerr and Eastern and Western Alyawarr. There are two smaller languages in the group, not so closely related: Kaytetye to the north and Lower Arrernte to the south. The territory of the group comprises very roughly the south-eastern quarter of the Northern Territory (of which a fairly big chunk, the Simpson Desert, is uninhabitable), and also extends into South Australia north of Oodnadatta . Alice Springs is in Central Arrernte country. There are about 4500 speakers of languages of the group.

Sounds

The Arandic languages are believed to have had sound systems very much like their neighbouring languages, such as Warlpiri and Pitjantjatjara, at some time in the distant past, but they've changed drastically over the centuries. As an example, the word wama ('snake') has become apmwe, apme and mwang in various dialects.

Vowels

The most common vowel in Arandic languages is written e, but its pronunciation depends very much on what sounds come immediately before and after. Other vowels are a (similar to the 'a' in 'father'), in some dialects; i (sounds like 'air' or like 'ee' in 'see', depending on what the next consonant is); and u (pronounced like 'u' in 'put' when it begins a word, or like 'or' in 'more' when it comes after the first consonant).

CENTRAL AUSTRALIA

Arandic Language Group

AUSTRALIA

LOCATOR MAP

Arandic
Language Area

Approximate Language
Boundaries Only

Based upon the IAD Language Centre map:
Current Distribution of
Central Australian Languages

0   100   200 km.

Stuart Hwy

Barkly Hwy

NORTHERN
TERRITORY

Tennant Creek

Camooweal

ALYAWARR

Mt Isa

KAYTETYE

Sandover Hwy

Neutral Junction

Urandangie

Yuendumu

ANMATYERR

Tanami Rd

Mt Swan

Plenty Hwy

Papunya

EASTERN
ARRERNTE

Alice Springs

QUEENSLAND

WESTERN
ARRERNTE

CENTRAL
ARRERNTE

SOUTHERN
ARRERNTE

Simpson
Desert

Lasseter Hwy

Finke

SOUTH   AUSTRALIA

Consonants

The consonant system is quite complicated, with a number of sounds that exist in almost no other Australian language. One unfortunate result, from the point of view of writing, is that some sounds which function as single sounds in these languages need to be written with two letters (such as nh, ly, pm, tn, rr) and some even need three letters (kng, tnh, tny, rtn).

Stress

Stress in Arandic languages is mostly on the vowel that follows the first consonant in a word, although in some dialects short words, such as artwe ('man') and iltye ('hand') are stressed on the initial vowel.

Structure

The languages of central Australia are basically similar in their grammar. The most obvious differences from English are the use of different endings on words where we'd use prepositions (like 'to', 'for', 'with') in English, and the fact that the order of words in a sentence is nowhere near as fixed as in English. The endings tell us which words in a sentence are the subject and the object, and so changing the order of words doesn't change the meaning as it would in English. The endings differ from language to language but the systems are much the same. The basic grammar of Central Arrernte is described in *A Learner's Guide to Eastern and Central Arrernte* by Jenny Green (IAD Press, 1994).

Arrernte Geography

The Arrernte name for the Alice Springs area is Mparntwe, while Heavitree Gap is Ntaripe. The MacDonnell Ranges as a whole are called Tyurretye (sometimes spelt Choritja). Prominent Central Australian mountains include: Rwetyepme (Mt Sonder), Urlatherrke (Mt Zeil) and Alhekulyele (Mt Gillen).

Other well-known scenic spots in Arrernte country include:

CENTRAL AUSTRALIA

Eastern MacDonnell Ranges

Anthwerrke	Emily Gap
Kepalye	Jessie Gap
Inteyarrkwe	Ross River
Ilwentye	Ndhala Gorge

Western MacDonnell Ranges

Urrengetyirrpe	Simpsons Gap
Angkele	Standley Chasm
Twipethe	Ellery Creek Big Hole
Kwartetweme	Ormiston Gorge
Yaperlpe	Glen Helen Gorge

Arrernte placenames are of two types. One type is when the name describes the place; for example, the Finke River is Lherepirnte (anglicised as Larapinta). This is composed of lhere ('river') and pirnte ('salt'), although there's some doubt about this, as pirnte means 'spring (of water)' in some dialects. Likewise, Finke is Aperturl, (usually spelled Aputula), which translates as 'hill-forehead' and refers to a nearby hill.

The second type of name is taken from the Dreaming (or Aboriginal creation history) of the area. For example, an area in Alice Springs is called Ntyarlkarletyaneme ('the place where the elephant grub crosses over'). Ntyarlke ('the elephant grub') is one of the ancestral caterpillar beings which created much of the landscape around Alice Springs as well as being a caterpillar that still occurs in the area. Some hills in the area covered by the name are parts of the body of these ancestral beings (see the signs at the golf course). Further east, in the MacDonnell Ranges, Anthwerrke, the name for Emily Gap means 'small intestine' and refers to the guts of the caterpillar.

Vocabulary

Some words that you may come across during your visit are:

arelhe/tyerrtye	Aboriginal person
lhentere/warlpele	non-Aboriginal person

altyerre	Dreaming, the Law
inernte	bean tree
urtne	coolamon (a shallow wooden dish)
irrtyarte	spear
alye	boomerang
atneme	woman's digging stick
kwatye	water
merne	food, especially vegetable foods and bread
utyerrke	bush fig
akatyerre	desert raisin
pmerlpe	quandong (edible fruit)
untyeye	corkwood
kere	meat or animal used for food
aherre	red plains kangaroo
atyunpe	perentie (large lizard)
rapite	rabbit
arlewatyerre	sand goanna
tyape	edible grubs
ntyarlke	elephant grub
yeperenye	caterpillar that lives on the tar vine
ngkwarle	sweet things
yerrampe	honey ant

References

The following books are all available through IAD Press and local bookshops – see page 164 for details.

Green, J 1993, *Alyawarr to English Dictionary*, IAD Press

Green, J 1994, *A Learner's Guide to Eastern and Central Arrernte*, IAD Press

Henderson, J 1991, *A Learner's Wordlist of Eastern and Central Arrernte*, IAD Press

Henderson, J & Dobson, V 1994, *Eastern and Central Arrernte to English Dictionary*, IAD Press

Swan, C & Cousens, M 1993, *A Learner's Wordlist of Pertame*, IAD Press

The Arrernte Landscape of Alice Springs by David Brooks (IAD Press, 1991) gives readers an insight into the traditional history of Mparntwe (Alice Springs), and offers a fascinating travelogue of the Alice Springs region. To follow the text of the booklet, readers need to climb Anzac Hill and Annie Meyer Hill to get a view over the town area. *Arrernte Foods: foods from Central Australia* by Margaret-Mary Turner (IAD Press, 1994), an Arrernte woman takes a comprehensive look at traditional bush foods from Mparntwe and surrounding areas.

WESTERN DESERT LANGUAGE
Languages & Dialects

The Western Desert Language spreads over a vast area of desert country (see map, page 172). Dialects of Western Desert include Pitjantjatjara, Yankunytjatjara, Ngaanyatjarra, Ngaatjatjarra, Pintupi, Papunya Luritja, Luritja, Matutjara, Kukatja, Antikirinya, Mantjiltjara and Kartutjara.

In all, it's estimated that there are between 4000 and 5000 speakers of Western Desert dialects, with Pitjantjatjara being one of the better known varieties. Most of the Pitjantjatjara and Yankunytja-tjara people live on the Anangu Pitjantjatjara freehold lands in the north-west of South Australia, or just over the borders in Western Australia and the Northern Territory.

Visitors to central Australia are likely to meet speakers of Pitjantjatjara and Yankunytjatjara at Uluru (Ayers Rock) and Kata Tjuta (the Olgas), and Pitjantjatjara and Luritja speakers at Watarrka (Kings Canyon).

Sounds

The examples of sounds given here are all from Pitjantjatjara or Yankunytjatjara. All other Western Desert dialects also contain these sounds, although there are some minor variations in spelling and pronunciation.

Vowels

Dialects of Western Desert contain three vowel sounds: a, i and u. These are like the sounds in 'father', 'hid' and 'put' in standard Australian English. Each sound may vary slightly according to the surrounding consonants. Long varieties of each vowel sound are written as aa, ii and uu.

Consonants

As with all central Australian languages, there are sounds in Western Desert language that aren't found in English. Probably one of the hardest sounds for the English speaker to produce is the ng sound when it occurs at the beginning of a word such as ngura 'home' or 'camp'. This isn't pronounced with a hard g sound as in 'finger', but like the ng in the middle of 'singer'. The underlined letters indicate retroflex or 'r-coloured' sounds (see page 177). There are several other consonant sounds that you may find tricky. It's not possible to learn to pronounce words correctly from the spelling without first learning by listening carefully to a speaker of the language, rather than learning from a book.

Stress

Stress in Western Desert dialects usually falls on the first syllable of a word. In long words, other syllables may also be stressed, but never as much as the first syllable.

Structure

Most dialects of Western Desert have a similar or related structure, but use different vocabulary, and some different forms of grammatical endings. The most obvious difference between the structure of these dialects and English is in word order and the use of case markers. Where word order is significant in English to mark subject and object, Western Desert dialects use case markers to mark subject and object. This means that word order is much freer than it is in English. Other elements of structure are too complex to describe here, but there are several reference books available through IAD to assist language learners.

Western Desert Language Group

Western Desert Language Area
Approximate Language Boundaries Only

Based upon the IAD Language Centre map:
Current Distribution of Central Australian Languages

Uluru & Kata Tjuta

Both of these landmarks are on the border between Pitjantjatjara and Yankunytjatjara country. The name Uluru is thought by some people to be derived from ulerenye, an Arrernte word for 'stranger'. Kata Tjuta translates into English as 'heads' or 'many heads'. There are signs around the base of Uluru and at Kata Tjuta in Pitjantjatjara, with English translations. An excellent way to learn more about the language and culture is to take the Liru Walk or one of the other guided walks run by the Australian Nature Conservation Agency.

Pitjantjatjara and Yankunytjatjara people call tourists minga tjuta ('ants'). If you stand at the base of Uluru, and watch people climbing you'll understand why. Although it's not widely advertised, the traditional owners of Uluru would prefer that you didn't climb the rock. There's a sign explaining this at the base of the climb. Apart from the damage being caused to sacred sites, the traditional owners are worried about the number of people that have been killed or injured during the climb.

Vocabulary

Some words that you may come across during your visit are:

anangu	Aboriginal person
piranpa/walypala	non-Aboriginal person
tjukurpa	Dreaming, the Law
ininti	bean tree
piti	coolamon (wooden bowl used to carry water)
katji/kulata	spear
kali	boomerang
wana	women's digging stick
kapi	water
mai	food, especially vegetable foods and bread
ili	bush fig
kampurarpa	desert raisin

wayanu	quandong
witjinti	corkwood
kuka	meat or animal used for food
malu	red plains kangaroo
ngintaka	perentie
rapita	rabbit
tinka	sand goanna
anumara	edible caterpillar
maku	edible grubs, especially witchetty grub (grub that lives in the roots of the witchetty bush)
wama	sweet things, nowadays also used to refer to alcohol
tjala	honey ant
kurku	honeydew on mulga (an acacia shrub)

Watarrka

Watarrka (Kings Canyon) is in Luritja country, and takes its name from a type of acacia known as the umbrella bush (Acacia ligulata) that grows in the valley below the canyon. There are signs around the canyon walk in Pitjantjatjara, with English translations. You can learn more about the language and culture of people from this area by taking one of the tours organised by Kurkara Tours based at the resort (Kings Canyon Frontier Lodge).

References

The following books are all available through IAD Press and local bookshops – see page 164 for details.

Eckert, P & Hudson, J *Wangka Wiru: A handbook for the Pitjantjatjara language learner,* University of South Australia

Goddard, C 1992, *Pitjantjatjara/Yankunytjatjara to English Dictionary,* IAD Publications

Hansen, K.C. & L.E. 1992, *Pintupi/Luritja Dictionary,* IAD Publications

Amee Glass has written a booklet called *Into Another World: A glimpse of the Culture of the Ngaanyatjarra People of Central Australia* (IAD Press, 1993) about living with Ngaanyatjarra people from Warburton, which is just over 200 kilometres west of the Northern Territory border in Western Australia. This booklet contains some very useful information, much of which is also relevant to relating to people from other language groups, particularly other Western Desert languages.

WARLPIRI
Languages & Dialects

Warlpiri is part of the Ngarrkic language group (see map, page 176). There are thought to be at least 3000 Warlpiri speakers, most of whom speak Warlpiri as their first language. They live in a number of quite large communities around the edge of traditional Warlpiri country: Yurntumu (Yuendumu), Lajamanu (which used to be called Hooker Creek, and is actually on Kurindji country), Wirliyajarrayi (Willowra) and Nyirrpi (which is strictly speaking a Pintupi community). But many Warlpiri spend at least part of the year in the many small out-stations in Warlpiri country, the heart of which is the Tanami Desert, named by Europeans after Janami rockhole, near the junction of the Tanami road and the Lajamanu road. There are also very substantial Warlpiri populations in other communities around traditional Warlpiri country, especially Alekarenge on Kaytetye country (a Kaytetye name referring to *Dog Dreaming*, also written Ali Curung and which used to be called Warrabri), and in towns such as Alice Springs on Arrernte country, Tennant Creek on Warumungu country, and Katherine on Jawoyn country.

Warlpiri is still a very vigorous language, and though it's being lost by Warlpiri children in some communities that lie outside the traditional country, usually to Aboriginal English or an Aboriginal creole, it's nonetheless spreading well outside its traditional country, and is also spoken by 1000 or more people as a second language over a very large area, extending as far north as Darwin, west to Fitzroy crossing in WA, east to Tennant creek and other Barkly Tableland communities, and south to Alice Springs and the northern Western Desert communities.

There are five major dialects of Warlpiri: Warrmarla or Ngardilypa was spoken to the west, Warnayaka to the north,

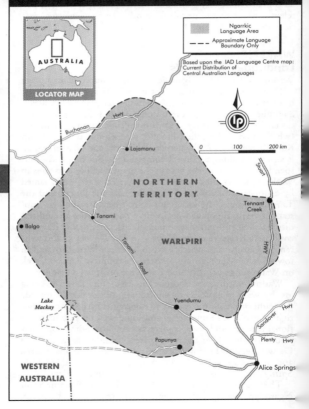

Ngaliya to the south, Yarlpiri or Warlpiri in the Lander River area in the heart of Warlpiri country, and Wakirti Warlpiri in the Hansen River area to the east. The main differences are in vocabulary and pronunciation, reflecting the influences of neighbouring languages, but they are mutually comprehensible. Though the Warlpiri will sometimes emphasise the dialect differences, they generally consider themselves to be one people with one language, Warlpiri.

Warlpiri has a spelling system which has been in use since 1974, mainly in the context of bilingual education programs in the schools of the main Warlpiri communities. Nowadays, most young and even middle-aged Warlpiri can read and write their language.

Vowels

Warlpiri has only three vowels, written i, u and a. The u sound has the European pronunciation, like 'oo' in 'zoo'. Long varieties of each vowel sound are written as ii, uu and aa.

Consonants

The 'retroflex' sounds rt, rn, and rl are pronounced with the tongue-tip curled right back, so that the bottom of the tongue tip touches the roof of the mouth. Warlpiri has three 'r's: r, rr and rd. The rr represents a trilled 'r'; rd is a retroflex 'r', made with the tongue flicked forward rapidly. The sound ng represents the sound in 'singer', never that in 'finger'.

Stress

Stress always falls on the first syllable of the word. Words in Warlpiri are always at least two syllables long, and must end in a vowel, so words borrowed from English can be quite hard to recognise; e.g. kuurlu ('school') and wijipirtili ('hospital').

Structure

Warlpiri has a complex grammar: for instance it has a case system (a set of categories for nouns, etc), five verb classes and a complex tense system. Although its system of counting is poorly developed, it makes extensive use of a distinction between singular (one), dual (two, a pair) and plural (more than two) in both the grammar and kinship system. There are several reference books available from IAD to assist language learners.

Vocabulary

Some words that you may come across during your visit are:

yapa	Aboriginal person
kardiya	non-Aboriginal person
jukurrpa	Dreaming, the Law
karli	boomerang
parraja	coolamon, used to winnow (separate grains and chaff), carry food, and as a baby carrier
ngapa	water
mangarriyi/miyi	food, especially vegetable foods and bread
ngurlu	seeds, grain
ngayaki	bush tomato
yarla	bush potato
kuyu	meat or animal used for food
marlu	red plains kangaroo
yankirri	emu
wardapi	sand goanna
pama	delicacy, nowadays also used to refer to alcohol
jurlarda	bush honey
ngarlkirdi	witchetty grub

References

IAD Press publishes Warlpiri learning materials, including *A Learner's Guide and Warlpiri Tape Course for Beginners* by Mary Laughren & Robert Hoogenraad (IAD Press 1996) and *An Elementary Warlpiri Dictionary* (revised edition) by Ken Hale (IAD Press). Warlpiri is probably the best researched Australian Aboriginal language: see Appendix II: Other Warlpiri Resources in the *Learner's Guide*, mentioned above.

TOP END LANGUAGES

The 'Top End' is a colourful term which can be used to refer to the northern half of the Northern Territory since it's at the 'top' of a map of Australia. Although it's a useful term to refer to this area on a map, it might suggest that the 'Top End' is somehow geographically and culturally homogenous, but this is definitely not the case.

The region encompasses a great variety of different environments – saltwater coastal areas, subcoastal flood plains, inland rock plateau and escarpment country, freshwater river systems, open savanna and grasslands and dry inland deserts. Each environment is populated with its own distinct plants and animals. Just as the country has influenced the type and diversity of plant and animal life in the region, so it has influenced in profound ways the life of its Aboriginal inhabitants: population density, the degree to which people were nomadic, hunting and gathering techniques and associated material culture, trade routes (and therefore the routes of diffusion for innovations in culture and language) and so on. Just as the country in the Top End displays great ecological diversity, so its Aboriginal inhabitants have many distinct cultural and linguistic traditions.

The Top End is the home of a great many Aboriginal languages. Some are related to other languages traditionally spoken on the Australian mainland, like the Yolŋu languages of the northeast which are related to Pama-Nyungan languages. (see page 150). Others belong to language families confined to the Top End, that is, to the various Top End language families collectively referred to as the Top End. Yet other Top End languages appear to be language isolates – unrelated to any other language of the region – for instance Tiwi spoken on Bathurst and Melville Islands. Members of a particular language grouping may speak a distinct language or they may speak a distinctive dialect. In the latter case, they will understand the speakers of the other dialects within that language grouping.

Regardless of the 'comprehensibility distance' between language varieties, membership in a particular language is of great social and cultural significance. Land, language and people are inextricably bound together in Aboriginal culture. Traditionally, languages belong to tracts of country (often having been put in their places by Dreamtime creator figures) therefore Aboriginal people belong to their country and to their languages. Ownership of particular country and its associated language is inherited through either or both parents, depending on the area. With this comes the birthright to particular language(s) and dialect(s).

Travellers in the Top End are often intrigued by the numbers of languages represented in this region, but really this is a matter of 'relativity'. Linguistic situations comparable or even more diverse to that found in the Top End can be seen in the tropics north of Australia. The island containing Irian Jaya and Papua New Guinea, for example, contains 20% of the world's languages.

Following are some cross-cultural hints relevant for those travelling in the Top End (see page 157 for more cross-cultural information):

- many Aboriginal people don't speak standard Australian English
- conversational styles differ cross-culturally
- politeness conventions don't map neatly across languages and cultures
- what is considered socially appropriate behaviour obviously varies among people of different cultural backgrounds
- hearing the name of a recently deceased person (or viewing an image, hearing a recording, etc) distresses Aboriginal people close to the deceased
- family and 'skin' relationships play a primary role in most facets of Aboriginal people's lives

LAND RIGHTS

Much of the north-east of the Northern Territory is part of Arnhem Land, a reserve established in 1933 and granted Aboriginal title under the Aboriginal Land Rights Act (NT) of 1976. In recent years, many Aboriginal Language Groups have been able to claim (part of) their traditional lands through this Act. Due to the provisions of this legislation, about the kind of land able to be claimed and about who may be recognised as traditional owners, not all Aboriginal groups have been able to regain possession of their land. (The effect in the Top End of the 1992 Supreme Court decision on Mabo, which has finally recognised indigenous peoples' land tenure, is as yet unknown.)

It was in part the regaining of the ownership of and access to traditional lands which made the 'Homeland Centres' movement possible. (Homeland Centres is the term commonly used in the north-east region. In other areas, the term 'outstation' is in use – in some instances for the same kind of smaller community, in some instances for a less permanent 'base' in a group's traditional country.) This movement began in the 1970s and saw family groups opting to move out of larger communities to their tradititional lands to start 'Homeland Centres' with populations of 15 to a hundred.

It should be noted that access to Aboriginal land and communities is restricted and monitored by a system of permits. Intending visitors must apply in advance to the relevant land council or community council – the Northern Land Council for most of the Top End, Anindilyakwa Land Council on Groote Eylandt or Central Land Council for some of the more southerly areas.

HISTORICAL INFLUENCES
Macassans

During at least the last two centuries before European invasion, Aboriginal peoples of the north coast of Australia had regular interaction with people from further north. These people, known as 'Macassans' (from present day Sulawesi), came south every year for trepang – 'sea cucumbers'. The legacy of their visits is found in material items, family ties, language and ceremony. When Europeans first attempted to create settlements on the north coast near Darwin in the 1800s, they recorded that Aboriginal people addressed them using a Malay pidgin which had presumably been acquired through their long term contact with Macassans or other seafaring peoples from the archipelogo to the north. Words from Macassan are found in many northern languages. Examples from the Yolŋu languages include:

rrupiya	'money' (Macassan: rupiya 'money')
bathala	'big, important' (Macassan: bàttala 'heavy, big, onerous')
detuŋ	(pronounced diitung) 'buffalo' (Macassan: tèdong 'carabao, water buffalo')

The Macassan voyages ceased in 1906 when they were banned by the Australian government. In recent times, however, contact has been re-established. People from Yolŋu communities have visited Ujang Pandang ('Macassar') and met relatives there. In 1988, a prau (canoe-like sailing boat) re-enacted the voyages of old, bringing relatives and others from 'Macassar' to old hunting grounds and families in East Arnhem Land.

European Invasion

The history of the European invasion of the Top End is important to the understanding of the present linguistic situation. In areas where Europeans settled early and in large numbers, such as around the Darwin region and along a corridor extending southwards following the Stuart Highway, traditional languages are no longer spoken.

In the drier open savanna country, cattle stations were set up using the labour of Aboriginal people. Aboriginal station 'employees' – their wage and living conditions often amounted to little better than slave labour – had to be able to communicate in English. It's difficult to generalise on the effect that cattle stations had on Top End language groups. Where Aboriginal station 'employees' were predominantly from the same language group like Wave Hill Station (Gurindji language group) and Humbert River Station (Ngarinyman language group), it was possible for people to continue speaking their traditional language in some situations, such as in the camp or out bush. The seasonal nature of the work – there was little or no work available during the Wet – also meant that Aboriginal 'employees' relied upon their traditional knowledge to survive.

Around the Top End coastline, missions were established and their effect on Aboriginal language groups depended much on the individual institution and on the specific circumstances of the area. In some instances, missionaries forbade the use of traditional languages; in others, Europeans working with a mission were expected to learn the traditional languages. At some missions, the so-called 'dormitory system' was enforced whereby children were housed separately from their parents in dormitories. This was particularly disruptive to the transmission of traditional languages.

Further Reading

Lewis, Darrell 1997, *A Shared History – Aboriginal and White Australians in the Victoria River District*, Northern Territory, Create a Card, Darwin

Read, Peter and Jay (eds) 1991, *Long Time, Olden Time – Aboriginal Accounts of Northern Territory History*, I.A.D Press, Alice Springs

Rose, Deborah Bird 1991, *Hidden Histories – Black Stories from Victoria River Downs, Humbert River and Wave Hill Stations*, Aboriginal Studies Press, Canberra

CURRENT LANGUAGE SITUATION

The Top End languages provide examples of all possible post-colonial fates of indigenous languages – from no speakers at all to full use in all everyday activities.

In areas with large, long-term European settlement like Darwin and Katherine, the traditional languages are no longer spoken. Visitors to such places may hear traditional languages being spoken by Aboriginal people but these would be from other areas. In Darwin, this could be Tiwi from Bathurst or Melville Islands or one of the Yolŋu languages from East Arnhem Land, among many other possibilities. In Katherine, visitors might hear Warlpiri from the desert country in the far south-west of the region. This is because traditional Aboriginal languages are still spoken in geographically more isolated areas where contact with non-Aboriginal people has been most recent.

More isolated areas where traditional languages are still fully spoken include the Daly River Region south-west of Darwin, Bathurst and Melville Islands to the north of Darwin, the Arnhem Land Reserve to the east, Groote Eylandt in the Gulf of Carpentaria and the desert region at the south-western periphery of the Top End.

In many areas with a lot of non-Aboriginal visitors such as Kakadu National Park, Litchfield or Nitmiluk (Katherine Gorge), only older members of the Aboriginal Community know their ancestral languages fluently; younger people may well understand and use some traditional language but they mostly speak Kriol, a dialect of Aboriginal English or another traditional language.

Further Reading

Hartman, Deborah & John Henderson (eds) 1994, *Aboriginal Languages in Education*, I.A.D. Press, Alice Springs

McKay, Graham 1996, *The Land Still Speaks – Review of Aboriginal and Torres Strait Islander Language Maintenance and Development Needs and Activities*, Commissioned Report No. 44 of National Board of Employment, Education and Training, Australian Government Printing Service, Canberra

Schmidt, Annette 1990, *The Loss of Australia's Aboriginal Language Heritage*. Aboriginal Studies Press, Canberra

Walsh, Michael and Colin Yallop (eds.) 1993, *Language and Culture in Aboriginal Australia*, Aboriginal Studies Press, Canberra

Language Shift

Establishment of large permanent communities this century through missions, reserves or cattle stations and in more recent times Aboriginal communities (small townships) has seen shifts in the traditional use and acquisition of languages. Although in some remote areas linguistic diversity is maintained, in most of the larger communities one language has become the language of common use. This may be a local language, Kriol or a koine, a new local language resulting from contact of traditional languages. As traditional languages are intrinsic to Aboriginal people's identity – their connection to their country, their ceremonies and songs – there is widespread concern about the maintenance of traditional languages.

In communities where traditional languages continue to be used, some languages are growing in numbers of speakers while others are declining. This is due to language shifts from one traditional language to another, in part because of changing demographic patterns. Formerly, small numbers of people lived in isolated clan groups and this isolation fostered the maintenance of many distinct language varieties. These days, even in relatively isolated areas, people tend to live for at least some of the year at large regional communities populated by members of different language groups. In such multilingual communities there's a trend for one language to emerge as a lingua franca.

At Maningrida community, on the coast of central Arnhem Land, where there are members of at least eight different language groups, two of the local languages are gradually emerging as lingua francas: one used by people who affiliate with the 'west side' (Kunwinjku and its eastern dialects); the other used by people who affiliate with the 'east side' (Burarra). Children growing up at Maningrida tend to learn one of these emergent lingua francas because these are the languages which they hear spoken around them most often and which enable them to communicate with the largest number of people.

KATHERINE REGION

In the Katherine Region, Aboriginal people nowadays use the terms 'sun-go-down' (or 'sunset') to refer to the people, lands and languages in the western Katherine Region (approximately west of the Stuart Highway) and 'sun-rise' to refer to the east. This division reflects the perceived differences in the nature of the languages, in the groups they're affiliated with, in traditional culture, in climate and country and even in art styles. Abstract 'dot paintings' are typical of the western Katherine Region, whereas figures and lined artwork typify the east side.

Katherine

The township of Katherine is the administrative centre of the region and it's possible to find members of all the language groups of the Katherine Region there as well as many others from even further afield. Of the three Aboriginal languages traditionally spoken in and around Katherine, Dagoman is no longer spoken, Jawoyn is spoken only by some older people. Wardaman is slightly 'stronger' in that it's been transmitted to some younger people who speak or understand it. The Aboriginal language that visitors to Katherine will definitely hear is Kriol. With the exception of Lajamanu in the far south-west, Aboriginal communities have a variety of Kriol as a first or main language.

Sun-go-down

The country is drier here than elsewhere in the Top End. The Victoria River is the one major river system in the entire region. There are four main areas of Aboriginal population in the western Katherine Region: (from south to north) Lajamanu; Daguragu and Kalkaringi; Pigeon Hole, Yarralin and Lingara; and communities in the environs of Timber Creek.

Lajamanu is now a Warlpiri speaking community because white authorities moved large numbers of Warlpiri people (see page 175) away from their traditional homelands farther south and onto lands traditionally owned by Kartangarrurru and Gurindji people. At Lajamanu, children are still acquiring Warlpiri as their first language and the community has a bilingual program operating at the school. Kartangurrurru might no longer be spoken, but Gurindji is still spoken in the communities of Kalkaringi and Daguragu to the north of Lajamanu.

At Kalkaringi (the old government settlement of Wave Hill) and Daguragu (the old strike camp of Wattie Creek) Gurindji is still spoken, however the main language of the children and young adults is a variety of Kriol which is influenced by Gurindji. Even though children and young people speak Kriol much of the time, they mostly have a thorough understanding of Gurindji. The Gurindji people are famous for the Wave Hill Strike of 1966 which fought back at the shocking wage and living conditions endured by Aboriginal people working on cattle stations at that time and which eventuated in a fight for land rights. To the east of Gurindji is Mudburra which is spoken across as far as Elliott. To the west are Nyininy and Malngin, language varieties that are closely related to Gurindji.

Bilinarra country lies to the north of Gurindji speakers around Pigeon Hole and Yarralin communities. However, Ngarinyman is the main traditional language represented at Yarralin and it's spoken over a large area to the north-west as far as Kununurra and northwards to communities around Timber Creek.

Speakers of the following four main language groups have settled in communities in and around Timber Creek: Ngarinyman, Ngaliwurru, Nungali and Jaminjung. Traditional country for the Ngaliwurru includes the spectacular Stokes Ranges. Nungali appears to be a threatened language with very few remaining speakers. Jaminjung is spoken to the west as far as Kununurra and to the north in some Daly Region communities. To the west of these languages, two further language groups occupy country in the Northern Territory: the Miriwoong and the Gajirrang (also known as Gajirrabeng and Gajirrawoong), although members of these language groups mostly reside in Kununurra and nearby communities in Western Australia today.

Aboriginal Languages of the Katherine Region

TOP END LANGUAGES

MAYA

Pine Creek

WAGIMAN

JAWO

DAGOMAN Katherine

Katherine

YANGM

Fitzmaurice River

JAMINJUNG

GAJIRRANG*

MIRIWOONG

Victoria

WARDAMAN

NUNGALI

Timber Creek

NGALIWURRU

Victoria Hwy

River

KARANGPURRU

Amanbidji

NGARINYMAN

Yarralin

Top Springs

BILINARRA

Pigeon Hole

Hwy

NORTHERN TERRITORY

MUDBURRA

Kalkaringi

MALNGIN

GURINDJI

Buchanan

NYININY

Lajamanu

WARLPIRI

AUSTRALIA

LOCATOR MAP

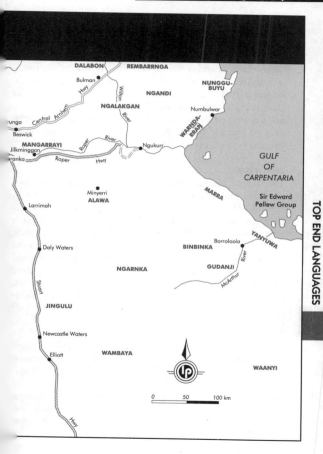

TOP END LANGUAGES

DALABON
REMBARRNGA
Bulman
NGANDI
NUNGGU-
BUYU
NGALAKGAN
Wilton River
Numbulwar
WARNDA-
RRAN
runga
Central Arnhem Hwy
Beswick
MANGARRAYI
Jilkminggan
Roper River
Ngukurr
GULF
OF
CARPENTARIA
aranka
Roper Hwy
MARRA
Sir Edward
Pellew Group
Larrimah
Minyerri
ALAWA
Daly Waters
Borroloola
YANYUWA
BINBINKA
GUDANJI
McArthur River
NGARNKA
Stuart Hwy
JINGULU
Newcastle Waters
Elliott
WAMBAYA
WAANYI

0   50   100 km

Hwy

Directly to the west of Katherine lies the traditional country of the Wardaman people. Most Wardaman people live in and around the town of Katherine nowadays. However, the Wardaman Association owns and operates Innesvale Station and there are also a number of small family outstations on Wardaman country. Wardaman was mutually intelligible with the traditional languages spoken near Katherine (Dagoman) and Mataranka (Yangman). Whereas Dagoman and Yangman are no longer spoken due to their location at points of early and extensive European settlement, Wardaman is still spoken and/or understood by some younger people today.

Sun-rise

The 'sun-rise' (eastern) side of the Katherine Region extends from the Stuart Highway across to the 'saltwater country' bordering the Gulf of Carpentaria. The environments pass (south to north) from the 'dry country' north of the Barkly Tableland, through to 'freshwater country' associated with the Roper and Katherine River systems and their tributaries, to the 'stone country' of the Arnhem Land escarpment. Major centres of Aboriginal populations include Borroloola on the McArthur River, Ngukurr on the Roper River, Minyerri (formerly Hodgson Downs), Jilkminggan at the headwaters of the Roper and the communities of Barunga, Beswick and Bulman on the Central Arnhem Highway.

Borroloola is situated on the traditional country of the Yanyuwa, although members of surrounding language groups such as Garrwa, Kudanyji and Marra all live in and around Borroloola nowadays. An interesting feature of Yanyuwa is that women's speech is structurally different to the variety spoken by men. Differences between these two varieties include a different system of prefixes so if a woman is talking about a male, she must use the prefix ny(a)- on the noun and any adjectives referring to him.

- woman speaking
  yenda ny-ardu nya-mordo
  you boy deaf (disobedient)
  'You disobedient boy!'

- man speaking
  yenda ardu mordo
  you boy deaf (disobedient)
  'You disobedient boy!'

To the north of Borroloola on the Roper River is the community of Ngukurr and several smaller communities and outstations. The linguistic situation here is highly complex. People affiliated with numerous language groups including Ngalakgan, Warndarrang (also spelt Wandarraŋ), Yugul, Marra, Ngandi, Alawa, Nunggubuyu, Ritharrŋu and Rembarrnga now reside at Ngukurr. Of these languages, Warndarrang and Yugul are no longer spoken, Ngandi and Ngalakgan have very few remaining speakers and Alawa and Marra are spoken fully only by some older people, while Rembarrnga and Ritharrŋu probably have relatively greater numbers of speakers in more remote communities.

Minyerri and Jilkminggan, communities further east in the Roper Valley, are on Alawa and Mangarrayi country respectively. The writings of Jeannie Gunn, such as *We of the Never-Never*, were based on her experiences of Elsey Station in Mangarrayi country. Mangarrayi, like Alawa and Marra mentioned above, is only spoken fully by some older people.

Barunga, Beswick and Bulman communities are located in Central Arnhem Land to the north of the Roper Valley on the Central Arnhem Highway. Barunga and Beswick were formerly part of Bamyili, a government reserve. The traditional owners for this country are Jawoyn. (The popular tourist destinations Nitmiluk (Katherine Falls) and Leliny (Edith Falls) are also on Jawoyn country.) However speakers from other language groups including Mayali, Dalabon and Rembarrnga also form a large proportion of the population at Barunga and Beswick. At Bulman, the major language groups represented are Dalabon and Rembarrnga which are spoken fully by some older adults, while younger adults tend to be able to understand their traditional languages but don't usually speak them fully.

Further Reading

Bradley, John 1988, *Yanyuwa Country – the Yanyuwa People* of *Borroloola tell the history of their land*, Greenhouse Publications, Richmond, Victoria

Fitzherbert, Sarah 1989, *My Dreaming is the Christmas Bird – the Story of Irene Jimmy* Bookshelf Publishing Australia, Gosford, NSW

Merlan, Francesca (ed) 1996, *Big River Country – Stories from Elsey Station*, I.A.D. Press, Alice Springs

KRIOL

Kriol is a new Aboriginal language that has upwards of 20,000 speakers spoken throughout most of the Katherine Region and the neighbouring Kimberley Region in Western Australia. The name 'Kriol' has been applied to it relatively recently and it has not yet gained widespread currency among all of its speakers.

As the name suggests, Kriol is a creole language – this means that it's a kind of 'emergency language' which has a specific origin. Kriol first arose early this century when surviving members of many decimated language groups congregated at the Roper River Mission in order to escape the brutal killings being carried out by cattle station companies in the area at that time. Many of the adults who came to the Roper River Mission were multilingual, but they were certainly not multilingual in exactly the same languages. Moreover, children had not yet developed full competence in as many languages as their parents. In this situation, the only form of language available for communication among everybody – including the English-speaking missionaries – was a pidgin that had entered the Northern Territory a few decades previously with the cattle trade and had become fairly widespread. Children acquiring language at the mission heard more of this pidgin than of any other language, not least because the missionaries housed them in dormitories away from their elders. The children acquired the pidgin as their first language and in doing so they created a full language which was able to meet all their communicative needs.

Due to its origins, Kriol has elements in common with traditional Aboriginal languages, with English and with other creole languages. As 'new' languages, creole languages tend to have fewer of the irregularities that occur in older languages and they also tend to convey most kinds of linguistic meaning with separate words. So whereas English can use the ending '-ed' to indicate past time, Kriol always uses a separate word bin to indicate an action happened in the past. For example, bin luk means 'looked'.

Traditional Aboriginal languages have played a very important part in shaping Kriol in its sound system, in many vocabulary items, in the meanings and in some structural features. Just like most traditional Aboriginal languages, Kriol doesn't use pairs of sounds like b/p, d/t, g/k, f/v, or s, z and sh to distinguish different words.

Pronunciation

All the letters used to represent Kriol sounds have their most common English values except for the following:

- a as in father
- e as in bed
- u as in put, bull
- i (mostly) like the sound in week, or (sometimes) as in tin
- o (mostly) as in port, or (sometimes) as in nod
- ai like the sound in shy
- ei like the sound in hay
- oi as in noise
- g as in go; never as in George
- th as in the, this etc; never as in thin
- rr is a flapped 'r' sound (a bit like the 'rolled r' in Scots English, Spanish, Italian etc)

Kriol speakers use large numbers of words from their traditional languages especially for domains of traditional knowledge like place names, traditional material culture, names for local flora and fauna and for personal information like Aboriginal personal names, relationship terms and body parts. As Kriol speakers who live in different areas draw on different traditional Aboriginal languages for vocabulary of this nature this gives rise to a great deal of regional variation in Kriol.

Kriol also uses many words that are more closely aligned with meanings represented in traditional Aboriginal languages – even if the actual 'shape' of the word is derived from English. So if a Kriol speaker talks about his or her mami ('mother'), don't be tricked into thinking the Kriol word has the same meaning as its close English counterpart. The Kriol item mami has the meanings associated with traditional Aboriginal kinship concepts. Although it can refer to the woman who bore the speaker, it can also refer to that woman's sisters, to her husband's brothers' wives, as well as to the countless classificatory mami (women who carry the same skin name as those female blood relations that the speaker calls mami) . In some ways Kriol also resembles traditional Aboriginal languages structurally. For instance, many traditional Aboriginal languages and Kriol don't have a separate class of 'adjectives' that enter into different structures to 'nouns'.

Nouns

Kriol uses a variety of markers preceding nouns to indicate plural number. However, there's a fair amount of leeway in Kriol as to whether plurals are marked or not – sometimes it's already obvious from the context if the reference is plural.

ola	*plural marker*
ola biliken	'the billycans'
ola kenggurru	'the kangaroos'

If Kriol speakers are referring to just two of something (dual number), they have to mark this with dubala (sometimes tubala). In Kriol it's ungrammatical to refer to two things just with the plural marker, unlike in English where indicating that there are exactly two of something is entirely optional.

dubala (tubala)   *dual marker*

dubala gel   '(the) two girls'

Verbs

Kriol indicates past time (past tense) with the marker bin before a verb (see Introduction of this chapter). This joins with the form im 'he, she, it etc' to make imin. Once a story has been established in the past, Kriol doesn't necessarily mark every instance of a verb with bin.

minbala bin wok gada ola biliken
'the two of us walked with the billycans'

imin laithad la melabat
'he said to all of us' [literally: 'he (was) like that to all of us']

Future time (and also necessity) are expressed with the marker gada (or garra) before a verb. This marker sounds the same as some of the forms of the word gada meaning 'with'.

yumob *gada* gu <u>gada</u> yumob matha
'you lot *will* go <u>with</u> your mother';
'you lot *have to* go <u>with</u> your mother'

Kriol has some interesting tools for indicating 'a lot of' an action or an event. These can be used independently or they can be combined with each other to achieve various nuances.

If something would occur regularly or habitually, Kriol uses the marker oldei 'usually, habitually, always, would, etc' (often shortened to ala). Oldei was originally derived from the English expression 'all day', but obviously doesn't have much in common with it now.

STORI BA HANTING GADA BILIKEN©

Melabat bin oldei gu fishing en hanting la Hadsen Riba. Mela bin oldei wok from kemp raidap la Ol Traking Yad. Minbala main sista bin oldei kadimap ola biliken.

'Wooow!' thad olmen bin oldei faindi maidi kenggurru la fran. "Shhh!" imin laithad la melabat. 'Shhh! Jidan kwait!' imin laithad. Minbala main sista bin thad tu las pesin. Minbala bin wok gada ola biliken: *durlurl, durlurl, durlurl,* meigimbat nois laithad. 'Gudnis! Yumob dali thad dubala gel ba jidan kwait gada them biliken! Ai gada trai shuda bif ba dina!' imin laithad.

Dei bin shat: 'Yumob yangboi, dali dubala ba shadap! Kadimap ola biliken kwaitbala!' dei bin laithad. Thed lil olgumen imin jingat 'Yunbala kadimap kwaitbala them biliken! Sowunso gada shuda bif ba wi iya'.

Bat minbala bin oldei wok-w-o-o-o-k: *durlurl, durlurl, durlurl.* 'Gudnis! Nomo yumob gada bulurrum mi hanting! Yumob gada ol jidan la kemp! Yumob gada gu gada yumob matha!' imin lathed, main dedi. 'Yumob nomo bulurrumbat mi hanting! Bikos ai kan shudim eni bif wen wi faindim'. Imin laithad du.

Thad trubala, orait. Im oldei gu hanting misel thad olmen en mela ol jidan la kemp! Laik ola lil drangkinmen mela bin oldei gu hanting. Mela bin gula-gula gija olawei: Thad olmen from fran im gula la thad olgumen. Thad olgumen gula la mela la bek! En ola kenggurru bin oldei sabi wen imin irrim ola tin: *durlurl, durlurl, durlurl,* im oldei gon! No kenggurru oldei lef!

© Maureen Hodgson, 1998

Acknowledgement

Adapted from a story recorded on 15 April 1998 by Maureen Hodgson at Binjari Community near Katherine, NT, as part of the research project: A Kriol Sketch Grammar – A Description of a Modern Variety of Kriol, supported by the Australian Institute for Aboriginal & Torres Strait Islander Studies.

STORY ABOUT HUNTING WITH BILLYCANS

All of us would go fishing and hunting at Hodgson River. We would all walk from the camp right up to the Old Trucking Yard. My sister and I would carry the billycans.

'Whoooah!' our father could, say, have found a kangaroo ahead. 'Shhh!' he would say to us. 'Shhh! Be quiet!' he said. The two of us, my sister and I, were the last two people. We walked with the billycans: *rattle, rattle, rattle,* making a noise like that. 'Goodness! You lot tell those two girls to be quiet with those billycans! I've got to try and shoot some meat for dinner!' he said.

They shouted: 'You boys, tell those two to shutup! Carry the billycans quietly!' they said. The little old lady yelled 'You two carry those billycans quietly! My son-in-law (literally: 'so-and-so', an avoidance term) is going to shoot some meat for us here!'

But the two of us would keep on walking: *rattle, rattle, rattle.* 'Goodness! Never again will you lot follow me hunting! You lot are all going to stay in the camp! You lot are going to go with your mother!' my dad said, he did. 'You lot won't be following me hunting! Because I can't shoot any meat when we find it'. He said that too.

That's true alright. He would go hunting by himself that man and all of us would stop in the camp! Like little drunks we went hunting. We were telling each other off all the way: From the front our dad yelled at that old lady. That old lady would yell at us at the back! And the kangaroos would know when they heard the tins: *rattle, rattle, rattle,* they would be gone! No kangaroos would be left!

> melabat bin oldei gu fishing en hanting
> 'we all would go fishing and hunting'
> 'we all usually went fishing and hunting'

If there's a lot of something happening – for example, when a lot of people are involved, or there's a repeated series of events – Kriol often doubles up (reduplicates) the verb.

> mela bin gula-gula gija olawei
> 'we were telling off each other all the way'

If something happens for an uninterrupted time span (especially when this is subsequently punctuated or terminated), Kriol speakers will often lengthen or stretch out a word as they say it. The pitch of the lengthened word is markedly higher than the surrounding words, so it sounds almost like singing.

> minbala bin oldei wok-w-o-o-o-k
> 'the two of us would keep on walking'

Kriol doesn't have any one item that's directly equivalent to the English verb 'to be'.

To indicate the meaning 'to be in a place or state', the Kriol verb jidan (sometimes also sidan) 'stay, stop, sit' may be used. However, where the orientation of something is important, such as vertical versus horizontal, or is inherent in its nature (for example, trees 'stand' in Kriol), Kriol always prefers the use of more specific verbs, like jendap 'stand, be vertical').

jidan kwait	'stay quiet, be quiet'
mela ol jidan la kemp	'we all stop in the camp'; 'we are all in the camp'

To express an equivalence relationship between one word and another (i.e. X is Y or X–Y), Kriol just places the items to be related together – with no intervening element.

thad trubala	'that is true'

Kriol remains primarily a spoken language, used for everyday communication in all-Aboriginal contexts. The popular Aboriginal band, Blekbala Mujik (as well as other bands from the Katherine Region) have used Kriol in their songs. However, it's also used as a language of instruction and in initial literacy work in the bilingual school program at Barunga Community where many Kriol texts for children have been produced. There's also a Kriol Bible translation and a Kriol-English dictionary.

Further Reading

Harris, John 1986, *Northern Territory Pidgins and the Origins of Kriol*. Pacific Linguistics Series C, No. 89, Australian National University, Canberra

Harris, John 1993, 'Losing and Gaining a Language: The Story of Kriol in the Northern Territory' in *Language and Culture in Aboriginal Australia, eds* M. Walsh & C. Yallop, Aboriginal Studies Press, Canberra, pp. 145 – 154

Sandefur, John 1986, *Kriol of North Australia: A Language Coming of Age*, Series A, vol. 10, Summer Institute of Linguistics – Australian Aborigines and Islanders Branch, Darwin

DARWIN & THE NEARBY COAST

Larrakiya is the language of the traditional owners of Darwin. Today it's spoken only by a few elderly people. For other languages of the Darwin region, such as Wuna and Limilngan, the situation is the same. You'll certainly hear many different Aboriginal languages spoken on the streets of Darwin, but none of them will be Larrikiya. The languages you'll hear will be indigenous to other areas, spoken by people who are immigrants or visitors to town. Members of the Larrikiya community are currently working to record and revive their ancestral language. Larrikiya words are used in songs written and performed by the Darwin group, the Mills Sisters.

Tiwi continues to be spoken on Bathurst and Melville Islands immediately to the north of Darwin. Bathurst Island is a popular tourist destination and texts produced in Tiwi language are available for purchase by visitors. Traditional Tiwi is a highly complex language although under pressures from colonisation, new less morphologically complex varieties of Tiwi – those having less word 'add-ons' – have arisen.

Along the coast to the east of Darwin are several different groups of languages. Very little is known about any of the languages spoken between Darwin and Kakadu. Only very old people still speak the languages of Kakadu and the Gurig Peninsula; most younger people now speak Mayali/Kunwinjku. On the islands off the coast, Iwaja and Mawng are spoken. Kunbarlang is a coastal relative of Kunwinjku and was spoken west of the Liverpool River, however most young Barlang people now speak Kunwinjku. There's a small language group comprising distant relatives of the Kunwinjkuan language family spoken in the area around Maningrida in central coastal Arnhem Land between the Liverpool and Blyth Rivers. The languages in this group are Ndjébbana (also called Kunibidji), Nakkara, Burarra, Gun-nartpa and Gurrgoni.

NORTHERN CENTRAL REGION

Most of the languages spoken in the interior part of the Top End are related to one another as members of the Kunwinjkuan family. Languages in this family include Warray, Jawoyn, Bininj Kunwok (dialects include Mayali, Kunwinjku, Kuninjku, Kune), Kunbarlang, Rembarrnga, Dalabon (also called Dangbon and Ngalkbon), Ngalakgan, Ngandi and Ngunggubuyu. Kunwinjkuan languages are spoken around the Arnhem Land Escarpment.

Warray is spoken by a few elderly people in the Pine Creek area. Jawoyn is spoken by some older people in Katherine, Pine Creek, Barunga and Beswick, around the south-western edge of the escarpment. Bininj Kunwok – literally, 'people's language'– is a series of dialects spoken in a chain around the western and northern rim of the escarpment: these are called Mayali in the west, Kunwinjku in the north-west (Gunbalanya area), Kuninjku in the Liverpool River area and Kune on the eastern rim of the escarpment.

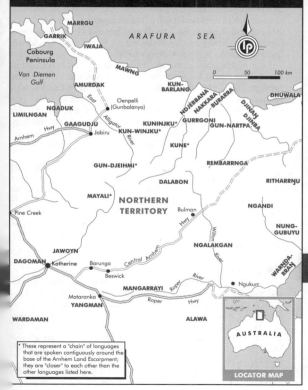

Aboriginal Languages of North Central Top End

ARAFURA SEA

MARRGU

GARRIK

IWAJA

Cobourg Peninsula

Van Diemen Gulf

MAWNG

AMURDAK

KUN-BARLANG

NDJEBBANA

NAKKARA

BURARRA

DHUWALA

DJINAN

DJINBA

LIMILNGAN

NGADUK

GAAGUDJU

KUNINJKU*

GURRGONI

GUN-NARTPA

Oenpelli (Gunbalanya)

Jabiru

KUN-WINJKU*

KUNE*

REMBARRNGA

RITHARRNU

GUN-DJEIHMI*

DALABON

NGANDI

MAYALI*

NORTHERN TERRITORY

Bulman

NUNG-GUBUYU

Pine Creek

JAWOYN

NGALAKGAN

WARNDA-RRAY

DAGOMAN

Katherine

Barunga

Central Arnhem Hwy

Beswick

Ngukurr

MANGARRAYI

Roper River

Mataranka

Roper Hwy

WARDAMAN

YANGMAN

ALAWA

AUSTRALIA

LOCATOR MAP

TOP END LANGUAGES

* These represent a "chain" of languages that are spoken contiguously around the base of the Arnhem Land Escarpment; they are "closer" to each other than the other languages listed here.

0   50   100 km

Dalabon, also known as Dangbon and Ngalkbon, and Rembarrnga are traditionally spoken around the eastern edge of the escarpment. Dalabon and Rembarrnga are today spoken on the northern rim of the escarpment at Homeland Centres such as Korlobidahda, Buluh Ka-rduru and Malnjangarnak, and also at communities situated south of the escarpment such as Bulman, Beswick and Barunga. Both the Ngalakgan and Ngandi languages, once spoken to the south-east toward the Roper River region, are today spoken by just a few elderly people.

Maningrida is an important regional centre and is situated in a transitional area between east and west Arnhem Land. There are significant cultural differences between Arnhem Landers who affiliate with the 'west side' and those who affiliate with the 'east side'. Burarra people affiliate with the 'east side' and the 'Burarra language has been used in popular music recently recorded by the Maningrida Sunrize Band. A variety of Bininj Kunwok is the language for inhabitants of Maningrida who are affiliated with the 'west side'.

Kunwinjkuan languages are famous because of the way that their words are constructed. In these languages words have a root and lots of 'add-on' bits called affixes that add extra components of meaning. Sometimes a single word is equivalent to a whole sentence in English. Some of the affixes go on the front of the word (prefixes) while other affixes go on the end of the word (suffixes). In Kunwinjkuan languages the prefixes are especially complex and interesting.

Noun Class

Most Kunwinjkuan languages have a system of 'grammatical gender' which linguists call noun class. In a language with a grammatical gender system, nouns make other words, such as adjectives, agree with them. (French and German, for instance, also have noun class systems. French has two classes, 'masculine' and 'feminine', German also has a third, 'neuter'.) Most of the Kunwinjkuan noun class languages have four classes, 'masculine', 'feminine', 'plant' and 'inanimate'.

Here are examples of noun class agreement in Kunbarlang. Each adjective carries a prefix that agrees with the class of the noun:

barbung *na*-rleng fish *masculine*-lots	lots of fish
balbarlak *ki*-rleng crab *feminine*-lots	lots of crabs
*ma*rdugudj *ma*-rleng plum *plant*-lots	lots of plums
*ku*walak *ku*-rleng rock *inanimate*-lots	lots of rocks

Noun Incorporation

Another characteristic of Kunwinjkuan languages is the incorporation of generic nouns into the middle of other words such as adjectives and verbs. The incorporated noun fits between the agreement prefix and the word root. Here are some examples of noun incorporation in Kunbarlang adjectives:

kirdimarrk na-*kuk*-karlyung man *masculine-body*-long	a tall man
momberk kinj-*kodj*-burrinj woman *feminine-head*-pleasant	a gracious woman
mardugudj man-*manj*-burrinj plum *plant-flavour*-pleasant	sweet plums
lorre ku-*lerre*-warri ground *inanimate-surface*-bad	uneven ground

Verb Agreement

In all Kunwinjkuan languages, verbs carry prefixes that give information about the participants, that is the Subject ('doer') and the Object ('done to'). The prefixes show person and number (I, we, they etc) and in some languages they additionally show noun class. The example below comes from Kuninjku, a north-eastern dialect of Bininj Kunwok:

Djaddi *ka*-yo kure ku-kurlk, ku-ronj, ku-rrulk.
frog he-lies on ground, in water, in hollows in trees
The frog lives on the ground, in water, in hollows in trees.

Ka-djare *ka*-ngun man-me yiman dumdum, birndu, bod.
he-likes he-it-eats food like beetle, mosquito, fly.

It likes to eat foods like beetles, mosquitoes, flies.

Other Prefixes

Verbs in Kunwinjkuan languages also carry other 'optional extra' prefixes. Sometimes they have a noun incorporated inside the stem:

Ku-djewk, djaddi ka-*rrabu*-ngukdeng ku-ronj.
rainy season, frog he-it-egg-lays in water

During the rainy season, frog lays its eggs in water.

Other prefixes can be used to add a participant. One of these is the Kuninjku prefix -ki- which means something like 'with'. In the following example, the -ki- prefix appears together with an incorporated noun:

Djaddi ka-wok-ki-yo. Bu man-djewk kabi-bun ka-wokdi
'ngukwong ngukwong ngukwong'

frog he-words-with-is if rain it-him-disturbs he-says
'ngukwong ngukwong ngukwong'

The frog is talkative. If rain disturbs him he says 'croak croak croak'.

Verb stems can also contain quantifiers and adverbs. Speakers of western dialects like Mayali and Kuninjku, enjoy constructing very long complex words. Speakers of eastern dialects, such as Kuninjku and Kune, use all of the 'optional extras', but usually only one or two at a time – not all at once. Even so, sometimes a single Kuninjku word is equivalent to a whole English sentence:

Birri-m-marne-kuyin-yawoy-yaw-kang (la birri-kodjkulu-boledkeng).

they-hither-him-for-nearly-again-child-took (but they-mind-changed).

They nearly brought the child back to him again (but they changed their minds).

Northern Kunwinjkuan languages (Mayali, Kunwinjku, Kunbarlang) have free word order in the sentence and no noun cases (marking on nouns to show how they're involved in the event) – all the work of tracking who's doing what to whom is done using the prefixes on verbs. Southern Kunwinjkuan languages (Warray, Jawoyn, Dalabon, Rembarrnga, Ngalakgan, Ngandi, Nunggubuyu) have case endings on nouns as well as prefixes on verbs.

Along the coast and the major river systems of the Top End (the Roper in the east, the Daly in the west) there's great diversity among language groups. Like the Kunwinjkuan languages however, they use complex systems of prefixes on nouns and verbs. However, note that Yolŋu languages are different in these respects.

THE DALY REGION

Languages of the Daly region, south-west of Darwin belong to several groups. Murrinh-patha has become one of the more widely spoken languages in the region. At Wadeye, one of the major communities in the region, members of eight traditional language groups moved in from their traditional countries to live at the mission.

Missionaries encouraged the use of Murrinh-patha, the language of the traditional owners of the country in which the mission was located. A Murrinh-patha bible was produced and linguists and language workers produced a dictionary and other documentary materials. Subsequently the school introduced a bilingual education program in Murrinh-patha. From the 1960s to the 1990s, Murrinh-patha gradually became the standard language of the whole community, arguably partly under the influence of its support by European institutions such as the Church and the school. An unintended side effect of supporting Murrinh-patha has been that few young people now speak any traditional language other than Murrinh-patha fluently and almost no children understand community languages other than Murrinh-patha. This is perceived as a serious issue by the community so the school and the local language centre have recently begun work on documenting the other community languages.

These languages have interesting grammatical features not found elsewhere in Australian languages.

Nominal Classifiers

Classifiers are words with a very general meaning, such as 'person', 'animal', 'long-shaped object', 'liquid', 'thing'. The grammar of these languages requires that every ordinary noun, such as the name of an animal or a variety of tree, occur together with a classifier. In several Daly languages, classifiers have a 'long' form and a 'short' form. The 'short' form joins on to the front of nouns and other words. The examples used below come from the Mati Ke language of the Wadeye area:

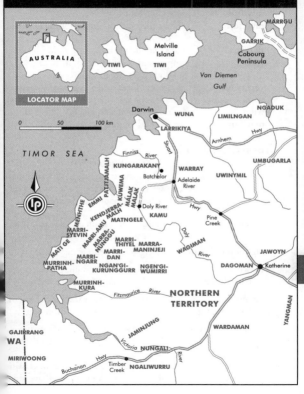

Aboriginal Languages of the North-Western Top End

TOP END LANGUAGES

meri/me-	higher animates; sentient beings (living people and spirits)
awu, a-	animals; people when you refer to them in a derogatory way
miyi/mi-	vegetable foods
nhanjdji	things (objects); natural substances (rock, sand, wind, sun)
thawurr	trees; wooden things; long rigid objects
yeri	implements of war and destruction (lightning, weapons)
yeri tjendi	spears and blades; all sharp-edged weapons
wudi	liquids (bodies of water, drinks, tea, beer)
wuyi	locations (times and places)
mati/ma-	speech and language

Cross-Classification

Some noun stems can be used with more than one classifier. Changing the classifier changes the reference of the noun. In many cases it's possible to see that the meanings of the two different combinations of classifier-plus-noun are related:

awu kulemin	long-bum ('animal'class); this is a mollusc, which is eaten
nhanjdji kulemin	long-bum shell ('thing' class)
thawurr babarlthang	red-flowering kurrajong tree ('tree' class)
nhanjdji babarlthang	string made from the inner bark of the red-flowering kurrajong
miyi babarlthang	edible seeds of the red-flowering kurrajong ('vegetable food' class)

In other cases the same noun stem is used with different classifiers and the different noun-plus-classifier combinations have quite distinct meanings. To a foreigner there may seem to be no connection between the two meanings, however there are often culture-specific conventions which link the two:

nhanjdji marri	cycad plant ('thing' class)
miyi marri	ripe cycad nuts ('food' class)
awu marri	bush cockroach that lives in dead cycad fronds ('animal' class)
me marri	a cycad/cockroach person; a person who belongs to the cycad/cockroach totem ('person' class)

A totemic complex links together people, animals and plants in culture-specific ways. In the Wadeye area, the cycad and the cockroach belong together in a totemic complex. To refer to a person as a plant or an animal is to refer to their totemic affiliation.

Fricative Sounds

Languages in the Daly Region have fricative sounds. These are made by bringing two parts of the mouth together so that they're very close but not quite touching; this causes turbulent airflow and a 'hissing' noise. (English fricatives are spelt with the letters 'f', 'v', 's', 'z', 'th', 'sh' and 'h', amongst others.) Of course, fricative sounds in languages of the Daly region are a little different than the ones we use in English. Similarly, the spelling systems used for Daly region languages are a little different to the English spelling system. The following are examples:

v there's no comparable sound in English. It's something like the sound which we write as 'v' and pronounced with the bottom lip against the top teeth, only this sound is pronounced with the two lips instead.

a-veng	agile wallaby
a-vu	brushtail possum
a-vandi	octopus

zr	this is something like the sound which we write as 'z', pronounced with the tongue tip curled right back

ma-zretja	relative, countryman
a-zramu	long-necked turtle
a-mizren	brahminy kite

dh	this sound is made by pushing the blade of the tongue up behind the top teeth. This sounds like the 'th' sound in 'there' or the middle sound in 'other'.

a-dhenirr	frill-necked lizard
a-dhazru	king brown snake
a-malidharr	bandicoot

zj	this sounds like the middle sound in 'vision' and 'pleasure' – push the blade of the tongue up against the hard palate.

a-zjingi	freshwater crocodile
a-zjingel	murex shell (the animal inside)
a-zjamba	plover

g	to make this sound, lift the back of the tongue up against the the back part of the roof of the mouth. There's no comparable sound in English.

a-warrgi	mangrove worm
mi-gumbi	white bush apple
a-gilhgunjin	black flying-fox (a large fruit bat)

NORTH-EAST ARNHEM

The Aboriginal population in this region is distributed between eight main communities being Ramingining, Milingimbi, Gapuwiyak, Galiwin'ku, Yirrkala, Umbakumba, Angurugu and Numbulwar and numerous homeland centres. Most non-Aborigines in the region are there for work, either in Aboriginal communities (in schools, clinics etc) or in the two mining towns of Nhulunbuy and Alyangula. In the 1970s self-determination directed the political agenda subsequently an increasing number of Aboriginal people are now holding positions previously held by non-Aborigines.

The languages of the north-east corner of Arnhem Land are of the Pama-Nyungan type. They have become commonly known outside the region as the Yolŋu (yuulngu) languages. In this area, each clan claims to have a distinct language variety and there are some 50 clans. The relationship of these languages to each other is complex. A useful starting point is to think of a patchwork quilt in which some materials appear at different places in the quilt. Instead of materials imagine a network of lands belonging to different clans woven together by spiritual, ceremonial and linguistic threads made by the Ancestral Beings. Land, clan, song, ceremony and languages are all linked together in this image by the common patches or threads that occur on the quilt.

There's a local way of grouping different clan language varieties which parallels linguistic ideas of language groupings. This groups together different clan languages according to the word used for 'this' or 'here'. Clans such as Gälpu (Gaalpu), Rirratjiŋu (Rirratjingu), Golumala (Guulumala) and Wangurri use dhaŋu and clans such as Djambarrpuyŋu, Liyagawumirr and Djapu use dhuwal. These words are indicative of a range of morphological and phonological differences. Within the Yolŋu languages there are five or six of these larger groupings and it's these groupings that are shown on the accompanying map.

The Yolŋu languages in this north-east corner are surrounded by the non-Pama-Nyungan type. From the north-west these are Burarra, Rembarrnga, Ngandi, Nunggubuyu on the mainland and Anindilyakwa, the language of Groote Eylandt. To this day groups within a geographical area intermarry and children are raised with different languages spoken around the hearth.

In all communities the population is still linguistically diverse. Only one language in the region has no living speakers. The comments following about the most commonly used languages are to be understood in the light of the fact that all communities are still multilingual, although the population of speakers of several varieties is ageing.

TOP END LANGUAGES

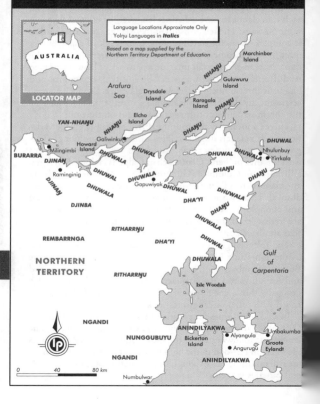

Aboriginal Languages of North-East Arnhem Land

Language Locations Approximate Only
Yolŋu Languages in *Italics*

Based on a map supplied by the
Northern Territory Department of Education

LOCATOR MAP

AUSTRALIA

Arafura Sea

Marchinbar Island

Guluwuru Island

Raragala Island

Drysdale Island

Elcho Island

NHAŊU

NHAŊU

DHAŊU

DHAŊU

DHAŊU

DHAŊU

DHAŊU

DHAŊU

YAN-NHAŊU

Galiwinku

Howard Island

DHUWAL

DHUWAL

Nhulunbuy
Yirrkala

BURARRA

Milingimbi

DJINAŊ

Raminginig

DJINAŊ

DHUWALA

DHUWAL

DHUWALA

Gapuwiyak

DHUWAL

DHUWALA

DHUWAL

DHUWAL

DHUWALA

DJINBA

DHA'YI

RITHARRŊU

REMBARRNGA

DHA'YI

NORTHERN TERRITORY

RITHARRŊU

Isle Woodah

Gulf of Carpentaria

NGANDI

NUNGGUBUYU

ANINDILYAKWA

Bickerton Island

Alyangula

Umbakumba

Angurugu

Groote Eylandt

NGANDI

ANINDILYAKWA

Numbulwar

0   40   80 km

The most widely spoken Yolŋu varieties are, moving from the west: Djinaŋ around Ramingining; a Dhuwal variety usually referred to as Djambarrpuyŋu (but somewhat different to the traditional Djambarrpuyŋu) spoken from Milingimbi to Gapuwiyak; Dhuwaya a koine (a new Yolŋu language) that has evolved around Yirrkala. At Numbulwar, Kriol is the first language of most young people but there's a major effort being undertaken in the community to maintain other languages, particularly Nunggubuyu. Anindilyakwa is still the first language of indigenous people on Groote Eylandt.

Traditional languages and culture are being supported by the schools in the region through various activities and programs. This has come at an opportune time for a couple of reasons. Firstly there are increasing numbers of Aboriginal teachers, including four principals, who can be proactive about local lan-

LANGUAGES & CLANS MAP KEY

Correlations between Yolŋu languages and Yolŋu clans:

Djinaŋ	Wulaki, Marraŋu, Murruŋun, Manyarriŋ, Djadiwitjibi
Djinba	Ganalbiŋu, Däbi, Mandjalpiŋu, Djinba, Walmapuy
Dhuwal	Djambarrpuyŋu, Liyagalawumirr, Liyagawumirr, Marraŋu in the west and Dätiwuy, Djapu, Marrakulu in the east
Dhuwala	Gupapuyŋu, Wubulkarra in the west, and Gumatj, Munyuku, Maŋgalili and Madarrpa in the east
Dha'yi	Dhalwaŋu
Djaŋu	Warramiri
Dhaŋu	Golumala, Gälpu, Ngaymil, Rirratjiŋu, Wangurri
Ritharrŋu	Wägilak, Ritharrŋu-Bidiŋal
Nhaŋu	Golpa, Gunbirrtji
Yan-nhaŋu	Gorryindi, Gamalaŋga, Mälarra

guage issues. Secondly, people still have extensive passive understanding of languages under threat. That is, they can 'hear' the languages even if they can't speak them fluently. Three communities have formal Bilingual Programs in which children are formally instructed in English and local languages.

Languages of the area have been written since the 1960s. Most writing is still associated with schools and bible translation. Bilingual schools have printing facilities so this is where most locally produced material is to be found. Some of these materials are available at local craft shops and newsagencies. Others are to be found as part of the Northern Australian Collection at the State Library of the Northern Territory in Darwin. The Yolŋu languages share a common orthography but different ones exist for the non-Pama-Nyungan languages of the region.

The Yolŋu have always encouraged people living in their communities to learn their languages. This ethos was even supported in mission times by the mission through an expectation that staff learn something of a local language. The rock band Yothu Yindi is probably the most widely known example of this willingness of Yolŋu to share their culture. The words yothu (yuuthu) and yindi translate as 'child, young' and 'big, important' respectively. However in combination they refer to the relationship between mother and child which extends to the clans, land and ceremony involved. The child's clan has major responsibilities to the mother's clan and members of the rock band are in this relationship to each other. Yothu Yindi draws its membership from clans associated with the eastern mainland communities of Gunyaŋara (Ski Beach) and Yirrkala. The lead singer Mandaway Yunupiŋu was named Australian of the Year in 1993 and their song *Treaty* raised awareness of land rights claims.

Another popular band in the region is the Wirriŋga band (Milingimbi) whose tapes are commercially available through CAAMA. Many other communities have local bands. Tapes of local church choirs are also available through local churches.

Further Reading

Groote Eylandt Linguistics 1993, *Eningerribirra-langwa lurra* (Anindilyakwa – English Dictionary), Groote Eylandt Linguistics, Angurugu

Heath, J. 1982, *Nunggubuyu Dictionary*, Australian Institute of Aboriginal Studies, Canberra

USEFUL CONTACTS

For further information on Aboriginal languages of the Katherine Region, you can contact Diwurruwurru-jaru Aboriginal Corporation (the regional language centre), PO Box 89, Katherine NT 0851 (tel. (08) 8971 1233, fax (08) 8971 0561, email: dactownling@nt-tech.com.au)

The Summer Institute of Linguistics (Australian Aborigines and Islanders Branch) has published many academic works and vernacular readers (both secular and religious) in a large number of indigenous Australian languages: Bookseller, Summer Institue of Linguistics, Post Office, Berrimah NT 0828 (tel. (08) 8984 4488; fax (08) 8984 4321; email: sildarwin@taunet.net.au)

Barunga Press, which produces Kriol literature for the Bilingual Kriol-English Program at the Barunga Community Education Centre, has a large range of reasonably priced Kriol booklets. Their address is PMB 117, via Katherine NT 0852.

FURTHER READING

Cooke, M. 1987, *Makassar and Northeast Arhem Land (Missing Links and Living Bridges)*, Batchelor, Batchelor College

MacDonald, E. 1964, 'Notes on the Noun Classes of Anyula' in *Papers on the Languages of the Australian Aborigines*, AIAS, Canberra

Urry, J. & Walsh, M. 1981, 'The lost 'Macassar language' of northern Australia', *Aboriginal History*, Vol. 5, A.N.U. Press, Canberra

TOP END LANGUAGES

Walker, A. & Zorc, S. 1981, 'Austronesian loanwords in Yol+umatha languages of northeast Arnhem Land' in *Aboriginal History*, Vol. 5, A.N.U. Press, Canberra

Zorc, D.R. 1986, *Yol+u-Matha Dictionary*, School of Australian Linguistics Batchelor, NT

TOP END LANGUAGES

WESTERN AUSTRALIAN LANGUAGES

As in other parts of Australia, there are two broad types of languages in Western Australia. Those which are spoken in the Kimberley roughly north of the Fitzroy River are of the prefixing type, like the languages of the Top End of the Northern Territory. The remainder are non-prefixing. (Prefixes are letters added to the beginning of words, used to distinguish types of words. See the Introduction of this section for more information.)

THE SOUTH-WEST

A single language, Nyungar, was spoken in the south-west of the state and existed in a number of different dialects. In the early days of contact with Europeans, a large number of loanwords were taken into English. However the effects of European settlement then caused a catastrophic loss of language (and culture), and there are now very few fluent speakers of Nyungar remaining.

THE MURCHISON & GASCOYNE

The main surviving language of this region is Wajarri, originally spoken in the Eastern Murchison. While there were a number of different languages spoken in this area, the people all referred to themselves as Yamaji and will say that they speak the Yamaji language. Wajarri is also spoken in Carnarvon where the original languages are essentially moribund. The eastern Wajarri people live in the Western Desert cultural area.

PILBARA

The southern and western Pilbara region, from the Gascoyne to Ashburton rivers formed a cultural area with the languages spoken along the Pilbara coast. The languages of this region also had similarities but, sadly, few speakers of these languages remain.

A number of languages are still spoken in the northern/eastern Pilbara, the most widely known being Yindjibarndi spoken in Roebourne, Onslow and other Pilbara towns. The Pilbara people form a cultural group sharing similar kinship systems and ritual practices. People travel from Carnarvon in the south, to Jigalong in the east and La Grange mission in the north for summer ceremonies.

WESTERN DESERT

A range of dialects of the same language are spoken across large parts of Western Australia, South Australia and the Northern Territory, extending from the Great Australian Bight, north to the Kimberley and west to the Hamersley ranges and Murchison goldfields.

KIMBERLEY

There were originally about 15 different languages spoken in the Kimberley region, but with quite a high degree of grammatical difference between these languages. The situation here is similar to that in the Northern Territory; while there are eight different language families in the Kimberley, the languages of the remaining areas of Western Australia fall into just one of these, the Pama-Nyungan family.

Most Aboriginal people over the age of 30 in the Kimberley, Pilbara and Western Desert regions speak one or more traditional languages. Throughout most of the state, Aboriginal people, except possibly the elderly, speak English. There's an array of varieties of Aboriginal English ranging from close to standard Australian English, through to varieties very close to Kriol (see page 192).

EFFECTS OF EUROPEAN SETTLEMENT

The European settlement of Western Australia began with the establishment of the Swan River colony (Perth) in 1829 and

spread to
other parts
of the state
over the next
50 years, with
the establishment
of pastoral industries
in the north-west, pearl
fishing on the Pilbara and
Kimberley coasts and gold
rushes in the Kalgoorlie and
Murchison regions. The effects of European settlement on
Aboriginal languages has varied from causing the gradual de-
cline in use over a number of generations, to rapid and complete extinction.

Knowledge of the Nyungar language has been gradually declining for 150 years. Today, younger Nyungar people may

WESTERN AUSTRALIAN

know little more than a few hundred words, and a handful of phrases. These are used to replace English words in what is otherwise a variety of Aboriginal English (see page 223). The original dialect diversity of Nyungar has been compromised, with virtually nothing remaining of the Perth dialect, and most people using words of the eastern Nyungar areas. English has had an influence on the sound system and grammatical structure of modern Nyungar. The initial nasal sound (ng as in 'sing') is not used by younger speakers, who thus pronounce words like nguup ('blood') as nuup. Younger speakers also use word order to distinguish subject and object, rather than the case-marking system of traditional Nyungar.

Language loss in other areas has been more catastrophic. Most of the languages originally spoken along the Ashburton river are now extinct, not because their speakers have shifted more and more to English, but because whole communities were destroyed by the effects of European settlement. The languages did not die, their speakers did.

In some places speakers of different languages were thrown together in organised settlements. Languages have been lost as people shifted to one or two main languages and away from their mother tongues. Yindjibarndi is the most successful survivor of the many languages which came together in Roebourne. In parts of the Kimberley, a new language (called Kriol) using words borrowed mainly from English, but with a sound system and some aspects of grammar taken from traditional languages, grew out of this situation.

KEEPING LANGUAGES STRONG

In recent years, many communities have increased efforts to maintain their languages and in some cases to revive languages which have been lost. An important part of this effort has been the establishment of community language centres which provide general language resource materials. The language centres encourage the interest of members of the general public and welcome visitors.

Aboriginal Languages of Western Australia

LOCATOR MAP

AUSTRALIA

0   400   800 km

KWINI
MIRIWOONG
WUNAMBAL
NGARINYIN
WORRORRA
BARDI
GOONIYANDI
Broome
NYIGINA
KIJA
JARU
YAWURU   Kimberley
WALMAJARRI

NYANGUMARTA
YULPARIJA

NYAMAL

NGARLUMA   NYIYAPARLI
PINTUPI
YINDJIBARNDI
BANYJIMA
THALANYJI

THARRKARI
MANTJILTJARRA
Pilbara
YINGKARTA
WESTERN
AUSTRALIA

WAJARRI
NGAANYATJARRA

NHANTA

WANGKATJA
Perth
NYUNGAR

NORTHERN TERRITORY

SOUTH AUSTRALIA

WESTERN AUSTRALIAN

Until very recently, Western Australia has not had a clear policy promoting the teaching of Australian languages in state-run schools and most language teaching or bilingual education programmes have been community based and privately or federally funded. Hopefully there will be an increasing number of state-run programmes in the future and a corresponding increase in awareness of Aboriginal languages in the general non-Aboriginal community.

Language maintenance and revival is closely tied to cultural maintenance and revival and an important aspect of this involves maintaining a spiritual connection to the land. In recent times, communities have sought increased control over their traditional lands. In some areas, people have moved back to their homelands and established 'outstations', in other places Aboriginal community groups hold pastoral leases and so retain access to their land for traditional purposes alongside the use of the land to run stock. Aboriginal rangers are increasingly involved in the management of national parks, and many communities continue to seek their rights to Native Title under federal and state law.

CULTURAL INFORMATION

The most important organising principle of Aboriginal society is the kinship system and every member of the community is part of a complex web of kin relations. As well as certain rights and obligations which stem from particular relationships, the system of kin relationships provides a safety net which is used by Aboriginal people when they are in trouble. Even far from home, the web of connections means that a person will be able to find a classificatory 'brother' or 'sister', a friend who will look after them. Aboriginal people travel a lot, and in WA can expect nearly always to be close to 'family'.

The kinship system determines various patterns of social responsibility, many of which require special forms and styles of speaking. Thus there are rules of politeness and avoidance; traditionally, people would avoid their in-laws and use a special vocabulary in speaking with them. Children would defer to members of their parents' generation, but interaction between members of the same generation, or between grandparents and grandchildren is more relaxed and often involves a great deal of joking, teasing and innuendo. Aboriginal people do not, as a rule, interrogate each other as English speakers tend to do, but rely on each other to be reasonably cooperative in communicating information.

Visitors can respect these rules of politeness by treating older people with respect and reserve and by understanding that the reserve they may meet from younger people is not necessarily a cool reception. Unless introduced, introduce yourself by first asking from a little distance, 'Can I come and see you?' Aboriginal people, both men and women, always take each other's hand in greeting, with a gentle and not too firm grip. They will usually expect you to introduce yourself first. The names of people recently deceased are avoided for a period of time and in general the overuse of personal names is avoided. People address each other by a kin term or by nickname.

Direct questions are easily interpreted as rudeness and are more politely phrased as statements of knowledge; 'I'm trying to find my way to the Language Centre'. More generally, if you want to learn something, give something in return. Tell a story/anecdote to hear a story. Don't be too serious, and don't be too surprised to find yourself the butt of a joke. Aboriginal people tend to tolerate more silence in communication than the average Westerner. If no-one says anything for a few minutes, don't feel compelled to fill the silence. Be content to wait and to listen.

As in most cultures, some knowledge is restricted and cannot be discussed freely. Certain rituals and particular sites, certain songs, dances and language styles may be restricted to initiated men. Some objects, decorations, or graphic designs may also be restricted and cannot be seen by uninitiated men and women.

All Aboriginal sites are protected under law, whether these are rock paintings or carvings, or scatterings of stone tools in a creek bed. It is an offence to disturb or remove artefacts found in the bush. While not all sites are specifically 'sacred sites', the land itself is sacred in the sense that Aboriginal spirituality embraces the land and everything above and below it. For Aboriginal people, the land is the source of their culture – the stories come from the land.

SPECIFIC LOCATIONS

The legacy of the Nyungar people is clearest to visitors in the host of local names for places, plants and animals found in the southwest. Aboriginal heritage trails giving details of the uses of various plants, the habits of animals, and historical and mythological information can be found in most national parks throughout the area. In the Goldfields, in communities across the Nullarbor Plain and in the desert, and along the Canning Stock Route north to the Kimberley, people speak dialects of the Western Desert language.

In the Pilbara, most travellers will visit the gorges in Karijini, the Hamersley Ranges National Park. This is Panyjima, Kurrama and Yinhawangka country. The Millstream/Chichester Ranges National Park is Kurrama and Yindjibarndi country. Aboriginal rangers from these local groups work in the parks, while local Aboriginal groups organise wilderness tours of Karijini, led by local experts.

In Broome, visitors will come into contact with speakers of Yawuru and probably also Karajarri, a Western Desert language. At Cape Leveque, tourists will most likely meet the sea-going Bardi people. Travellers on the Gibb River road will pass mainly through Ngarinyin country and visitors to the Bungle Bungle National Park, south of Turkey Creek will probably meet speakers of Kija and Jaru. Miriwoong is spoken further to the North, around Kununurra and Lake Argyle on the Ord River.

In the north of the state, especially in the desert, in the Pilbara and Kimberley, Aboriginal people often speak the new language Kriol, or Aboriginal English.

THE LANGUAGES

The sound systems of languages of Western Australia are quite similar to one another. Interdental sounds are made with the tongue between the teeth, alveolar with the tongue tip against the ridge behind the upper teeth, retroflex with the tip of the tongue turned back, and palatal with the tongue against the palate. While these sounds are found in almost all of the languages, there are a number of different spelling systems.

The grammatical structures of the languages vary. Nyungar, in the south, doesn't have complex suffixes and prefixes and, like some Asian languages, relies on sequences of individual words linked together to convey complex meanings and on relatively fixed word order. By contrast, the Kimberley languages have very complicated paradigms of word forms and in some cases a single word can express the content of a whole sentence. Throughout the rest of the state, words involve the addition of suffixes to indicate grammatical information and word order within sentences is often quite free.

Aboriginal people don't usually expect to speak their languages with non-Aboriginal people and in most such situations English is the language of choice. However, travellers who choose to try out a few local names for animals, plants, or places, will convey the message that they are interested in Aboriginal languages and sympathetic to Aboriginal culture.

Aboriginal English isn't always easily understood by speakers of other English dialects. Like Kriol, it uses sounds and structures that are borrowed from traditional languages. There are occasionally special pronouns, words borrowed from traditional languages (especially kin terms), and no gender contrasts ('he' and 'him' and words like 'fella', may be used for both men and women). Rules for use, politeness and avoidance, are like those of traditional languages. Visitors shouldn't try to speak Kriol or Aboriginal English. Because of the negative connotations of 'pidgin English', such attempts might be seen as patronising and insulting.

PLACE NAMES

Partiikunha	Clamina Gorge
Pajinhurrpa	Cossak
Karlayanguyinha	Cowera Gorge
Murlunmunyjurna	Crossing Pool
Mangkurtu	Fortescue River
Karijini	Hamersley Range (National Park)
Pilirripinha	Manyjina Gorge
Japurakunha	Marillana Gorge
Jintawirrina	Millstream Station
Kawuyu	Mt Nicholson
Walkartatharra	Mt Alexander
Pirnayinmurru	Mt Brockman
Punurrunha	Mt Bruce
Mukuriyarra	Mt Murray
Pirtan	Onslow
Kalharramunha	Rio Tinto Gorge
Jajiwurra	Robe River
Yirramakartu	Roebourne, Jubilee Pool
Kartirtikunha	Yampire Gorge
Parrkapinya	Whim Creek
Ngampiku	Wittenoom (Gorge)

The above list is composed of names from the Pilbara. Many place names in the south-west of the state end in -up. These are all original Nyungar names and the ending simply indicates that the word is the name of a place. Some examples of towns with this ending are:

Boyanup	Jerramungup	Nannup
Cowaramup	Kirrup	Porongurup
Dandalup	Kojonup	Quinninup
Dardenup	Manjimup	Wagerup
Gnowangerup	Mungallup	Wokalup

In the wheatbelt, a good number of names end in -n or -ng. These are also Nyungar names. Some towns with this kind of name are:

Burracoppin	Kellerberrin	Popanyinning
Corrigin	Kondinin	Quairading
Cunderdin	Merredin	Tammin
Katanning	Narrogin	Woodanilling

While some of these place names most likely 'meant something' rather than simply being names, it's not possible to know what this was without detailed knowledge of the exact named place and the mythology surrounding it. Resemblances to other Nyungar words is no guarantee of a connection in meaning.

FURTHER READING

For more information on the language and culture of particular areas see:

Mowarjarli, 1992, *Yorro Yorro*, Magabala Books

Richards E. & Hudson J. *Walmajarri-English Dictionary*, Summer Institute of Linguistics, Darwin

Thieberger N. & McGregor W. 1994, *Macquarie Aboriginal Words*, Macquarie Library, Sydney

Tilbrook, L. 1983, *Nyungar Tradition: Glimpses of Aborigines of Southwestern Australia 1829-1914*, University of Western Australia Press

Tonkinson. R. 1991, *The Mardu Aborigines: Living the Dream in Australia's Desert*, Holt, Rinehart and Winston

WESTERN AUSTRALIAN

LANGUAGES OF VICTORIA & NEW SOUTH WALES

The south-east of Australia, comprising the present-day states of New South Wales and Victoria, was the earliest and most intensively settled mainland area of the European colonies. During settlement the original inhabitants were dispossessed of their land and killed in large numbers through battle, the spread of disease, and the destruction of their environment and means of living. People were also herded onto missions and government settlements, sometimes being forced to live together with their enemies, and their traditional ways of life were prohibited. As a result, the transmission of traditional Aboriginal culture, including language, from one generation to the next was damaged and a great deal of knowledge was lost.

Today, in New South Wales, a few old fluent speakers remain for a small number of languages, including Bundjalung of the north coast around Lismore, and Baagandji, spoken on the Darling River near Wilcannia. No full speakers of a Victorian Aboriginal language are alive, and none of the languages is used as the main means of communication in any community. However, many Aboriginal people carefully preserve some elements of their linguistic heritage, even generations after the last fluent speakers have passed away. Today, words from traditional languages can still be heard in use in Melbourne and Sydney, and especially in country areas of New South Wales and Victoria. These words and expressions serve to declare the identity of Koori and Murri people amongst whom they continue to be used. In many communities there's rising interest in traditional languages and culture and efforts are under way to preserve and maintain the knowledge that remains.

Visitors to New South Wales and Victoria will see evidence of traditional Aboriginal languages in three areas: in the continuing use of Aboriginal language words and expressions; in names

VICTORIA & NSW

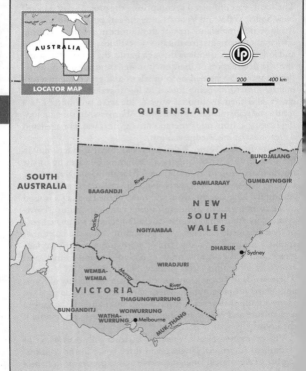

Aboriginal Languages of Victoria & New South Wales

AUSTRALIA

LOCATOR MAP

0   200   400 km

QUEENSLAND

BUNDJALANG

SOUTH AUSTRALIA

BAAGANDJI

Darling River

GAMILARAAY

GUMBAYNGGIR

NEW SOUTH WALES

NGIYAMBAA

DHARUK

Sydney

WIRADJURI

WEMBA-WEMBA

Murray River

VICTORIA

THAGUNGWURRUNG

BUNGANDITJ

WOIWURRUNG

WATHA-WURRUNG

Melbourne

MUK-THANG

Languages for which there's a deal of reliable information available include Bundjalung and Gumbaynggir (north coast), Gamilaraay (also spelled Kamilaroi), Ngiyambaa (or Wangaaybuwan) and Wiradjuri (north-west and central NSW), and Baagandji (or Paakantyi) (far west). Speakers of some of these languages remain and there are efforts under way in Aboriginal communities to revive and preserve linguistic and cultural heritage. Recently several excellent practical dictionaries and word books of New South Wales languages have appeared – these are listed in the further reading section at the end of this chapter. For further information the visitor is advised to contact local Aboriginal land councils, language centres and schools to discuss studies that are currently being undertaken.

Throughout New South Wales, as in Victoria, there are numerous placenames that have an Aboriginal origin. For many of these it's possible to give an interpretation of their literal meaning (although the significance of these names in the mythology and culture is often not available). Here are some examples giving the original pronunciation and meaning:

Boggabilla	bagaaybila ('place full of creeks')
Bundarra	bundaarra ('place of kangaroos')
Cobar	gubarr ('red ochre')
Coonamble	gunambil ('full of excrement')
Gunnedah	gunithaa ('orphan')
Nambucca	bagabaga ('knees')
Torrowotto	thuru-katu ('snake's windbreak')
Uralla	urala ('camp')
Wagga Wagga	waagan-waagan ('crows')
Woolgoolga	wiigulga ('black fig tree')

Many dozens of words from New South Wales' languages are now at home in general Australian English, especially for the names of plants and animals that were new to the first European settlers. These include:

- birds   galah, kookaburra, brolga, currawong, budgerigar

VICTORIA & NSW

- animals   dingo, koala, wallaby, wallaroo
- plants   mulga, coolabah, gidgee, bindi-eye
- landscape billabong ('river pool'), gibber ('stone')
- artefacts coolamon ('bark dish'), woomera ('spear-thrower'), nulla-nulla ('club'), gunya ('shelter')

FURTHER READING

The following are some introductory books that deal with Victorian and New South Wales Aboriginal languages. For more information contact: Australian Institute of Aboriginal and Torres Strait Islander Studies, GPO Box 553, Canberra, ACT 0200.

Austin, P. 1992, *A dictionary of Gamilaraay, northern New South Wales,* La Trobe University

Austin, P. 1993, *A reference dictionary of Gamilaraay, northern New South Wales,* La Trobe University

Blake, B.J. 1991, 'Woiwurrung: the Melbourne language' in *The Handbook of Australian Languages,* eds R.M.W. Dixon & B.J. Blake, vol. 4, Oxford University Press

Dixon, R.M.W., W.S. Ramson & M. Thomas 1990, *Australian Aboriginal Words in English,* Oxford University Press

Eades, D. 1981, 'Gumbaynggir' in *The Handbook of Australian Languages,* vol. 1, eds R.M.W. Dixon & B.J. Blake, Australian National University Press

Hercus, L.A. 1982, *The Bagandji language,* Pacific Linguistics

Hercus, L.A. 1986, *Victorian languages: a late survey,* Pacific Linguistics

Hercus, L.A. 1993, *Paakantyi dictionary,* Canberra

Sharpe, M. 1993, 'Bundjalung: teaching a disappearing language' in *Language and culture in Aboriginal Australia,* eds M. Walsh & C. Yallop, Australian Institute of Aboriginal and Torres Strait Islander Studies

TORRES STRAIT LANGUAGES

There are three Torres Strait Islander languages spoken by an Australian indigenous group of some 30,000 people, a large majority of whom are Melanesian people. The rest are of European, Asian and Aboriginal background. Their homelands are a group of small islands scattered along the waterway known as Torres Strait, between the tip of Cape York and Papua New Guinea.

Two of the Torres Strait Islander languages are original indigenous languages. They are Kala Lagaw Ya (KLY), spoken by the people of the western islands of Saibai, Dauan, Boigu, Mabuiag, Badu, Moa (Kubin) and Narupai, and the central islands of Masig, Purma, Yam and Warraber; and Meriam Mir (MM), spoken by the people from eastern islands of Mer, Erub and Ugar. Kala Lagaw Ya is believed to be related to Australian Aboriginal Languages. Meriam Mir on the other hand belongs to the Trans Fly family of languages along the Papuan coast.

The third traditional language of Torres Strait Islanders is an English-based creole, called Torres Strait Broken (TSB). It's an established lingua franca, mainly spoken in the Eastern and Central Islands and Thursday Island, and is the first language of most people there who were born after WWII.

About 6000 Torres Strait Islanders who live in the Torres Strait continue to use the languages and keep them strong. The remaining 80% of Torres Strait Islanders have moved to the provincial towns and cities in the mainland of Australia for various reasons, mainly in search of jobs, good health and better education for their children. Most Torres Strait Islanders who decided to move to the mainland have settled in the coastal towns and cities of Queensland.

Despite total exposure to the dominant western culture and English language, Torres Strait Islanders on the mainland have managed exceptionally well to maintain their traditional languages. Kala Lagaw Ya has about 3000 speakers while Meriam

Torres Strait - Inhabited Islands & Linguistic Boundaries

Australia-PNG Boundary
Major Linguistic Boundary
Dialect Boundary

PAPUA NEW GUINEA

LOCATOR MAP

PNG
AUSTRALIA

Daru Island

Boigu Island

Dauan Island   Saibai Island

Ugar (Stephen Island)

Erub (Darnley Island)

TORRES   STRAIT

KALA LAGAW YA

MERIAM MIR

Mabuiag (Jervis Island)

Masig (Yorke Island)

Mer (Murray Island)

Yam Island

Badu (Mulgrave Island)

Purma (Coconut Island)

Badu

St Pauls

Kubin   Moa (Banks Island)

Warraber (Sue Island)

Kiriri (Hammond Island)

Waiben (Thursday Island)

Narupai (Horn Island)

Great Barrier Reef

Muralag (Prince of Wales Island)

Seisia

Bamaga

Cape York Peninsula
Queensland
AUSTRALIA

CORAL SEA

0   25   50 km

Mir speakers are numbered close to 2000, and all Torres Strait Islanders speak Torres Strait Broken regardless of where they live in Australia.

In the Torres Strait today, people on central and eastern islands as well as on Thursday, Horn and Hammond Islands, use Torres Strait Broken on a daily basis, although most adults maintain their traditional indigenous languages. On Boigu, Saibai, Dauan, Mabuiag, Badu, Kubin, Seisia and Bamaga, Kala Lagaw Ya all have regular speakers. Meriam Mer on Murray Island is primarily spoken by adults. Thursday Island is a town with a mixed community of European, Asian and Aboriginal people. English is an official language and is used extensively in government offices, schools, churches, hospital and shops etc. While the two indigenous languages are often used by the speakers amongst themselves, Torres Strait Broken is the most commonly used language on Thursday Island.

EUROPEAN CONTACT

European contact has had devastating effects on the languages and culture of Torres Strait Islanders. The colonisation process and the cruel policies of assimilation, segregation and integration have greatly contributed to the marginalisation of Torres Strait Islander culture and languages. Official limitations were placed on the use of indigenous languages in schools and public places.

The impact of colonisation resulted in the creation of Torres Strait Broken as a new language in the area. It has developed mainly from the Pacific Island pidgin called Bislama which was brought to Torres Strait by Pacific Islanders who came to the area as labourers in the marine industry.

Interactions between Pacific Islanders, Torres Strait Islanders and other nationals who had migrated to the area, such as Japanese, Malayans and Chinese, resulted in the emergence of Torres Strait Broken which is now distinctly different from the Bislama as spoken today.

COMMUNITY & CULTURAL LIFE

The fundamental aspects of the original Torres Strait Islander culture have remained in tact, despite colonisation. However, since the time of initial contact, the dominance of European culture and the influence of other cultures that the Torres Strait Islanders came in contact with, have forced some changes to various aspects of the Torres Strait Islanders' culture. Thus it has been somehow modified and in some instances impoverished, although today, Torres Strait Islanders are still able to practise an enriched and unique cultural way of life.

The most notable cultural trait that Torres Strait Islanders on all islands have hung on to so tightly apart from their languages is their traditional dance. There are different styles of traditional dance which can be performed while standing upright stamping both feet, or in a sitting position. Both forms of dancing require a lot of hand movements and jumping. The dancers usually wear special costumes, depending on what the dance is about. To perform the dances the men wear a piece of cloth called lava-lava and a singlet, while women wear specially-made floral dresses. Also, the dancers equip themselves with special regalia consisting of grass-skirt, headress, headbands, necklaces, arm and leg bands and models representing the subject that the dance portrays. All dances are usually accompanied by singing and the pulsating rhythm of drums.

In May of each year, Thursday Island hosts the Torres Strait Cultural Festival. This is designed to promote and strengthen cultural identity. The activities of the Cultural Festival include traditional dance, traditional and contemporary singing, and stalls where people sell food, handicrafts, artefacts and carvings of all description.

Over the years, Torres Strait Islanders have developed a lifestyle suited to their environment. At one time they depended almost entirely on the sea for food and to travel from one island to the next. On land, they cultivated crops in their gardens and domesticated animals, mainly pigs. These days not much gardening is being carried out. Torres Strait Islanders rely more and more on community stores that provide general groceries, including fresh vegetables, fruit and meat. Fish is the staple food, and is caught by handlines and nets or hand spears, and is supplemented with rice, yams, sweet potatoes and taro. The important sources of seafood are dugong and turtle. Using traditional methods, Torres Strait Islanders spear them with a special harpoon. Because dugong and turtle are considered a luxury, people only eat them on special occasions like weddings and tombstone unveilings.

For special occasions, Torres Strait Islanders hold traditional feasts which include dancing, singing and lots of food. Traditional food requires a lot of preparation. One of the popular traditional foods is sop-sop, a mixture of vegetables chopped into small pieces and cooked in coconut cream. In just about every feast, food is cooked in an earth oven or kap mauri. The food for kap mauri is prepared and wrapped then placed on hot stones lying on the bottom of the pit specially dug in the ground. Any kind of food may be cooked in the kap mauri including vegetables, pig, dugong, turtle and damper.

Tombstone unveiling is one of the important family events celebrated with a big traditional feast. It involves a lot of preparation by the family of the deceased person. The preparations include the collecting of money from each member of the family, erecting a tombstone on the grave and putting on a feast.

The outer island communities are changing fairly rapidly from traditional village settings to small townships. All the islands now have modern houses, schools, medical facilities, telephones and electricity. However, in general, life on the islands is at a notably leisurely pace. The daily activities of the people revolve around family and community affairs.

Torres Strait Islanders are devout Christians. Most of them are Anglicans. Some islands have smaller churches of other denominations. They worship every Sunday in churches built by themselves. Church services are normally conducted in English but most of the hymns are sung in their own languages. An important religious event that people throughout the Torres Strait celebrate on 1 July each year, is the festival of the 'Coming of the Light'. This event signifies the arrival of the missionaries of the London Missionary Society in the Torres Strait in 1871. The festival is usually celebrated with a church service followed by a re-enactment of how the people on each island greeted the missionaries. In the re-enactment, some people dress as the missionaries while others dress in warrior costumes.

TORRES STRAIT LANGUAGES

The main authorities in an island community are the community council chairperson and the councillors, the priest and the clan elders. Visitors are expected to observe cultural protocol when visiting the islands. It's therefore important to find out as much as possible beforehand.

ON THE ISLANDS

The places that are visited most frequently by outsiders are Bamaga, Seisia and Thursday Island. In winter, tourists travel by road to Cape York and camp in the camping area at Seisia. A regular ferry operates from Thursday Island, to service the Northern Peninsula Area communities, on most days of the week.

Thursday Island is the commercial and administrative centre for Torres Strait. It has a fasinating history. The fort is one of the main attractions on Thursday Island. On Green Hill there are 16 inch guns which were build at the turn of the century in fear of a Russian invasion that never eventuated. Thursday Island is surrounded by a number of islands clustered together. The airport is on Horn Island and the airlines provide regular ferry services to and from Thursday Island.

All the islands not included in the Muralag (Prince of Wales) group, including Thursday Island, are referred to as outer islands. To visit any of the outer islands, it's important to make an arrangement with the Council of the island because of limited accommodation.

DIALECTS

Kala Lagaw Ya

Kala Lagaw Ya is a language with four dialects: the Kala Kawaw Ya (KKY) of the islands of Saibai, Dauan and Boigu; Mabuiag (M) of Mabuiag Island and Badu; Kaurareg (K) of Kubin (Moa) and Nurapai (Horn Island).

The differences between these dialects are minimal and lie mainly in words and sounds.

Meriam Mir

Meriam Mir (MM) had two dialects and the differences between them were restricted to words and sounds. Only Mer dialect has survived.

Variation in Torres Strait Broken

The way Eastern Islanders and Central/Western Islanders speak Torres Strait Broken (TSB) varies in terms of the vocabulary used, the different words being derived from their indigenous languages.

Awa, yumi go.	'Uncle, let's go.' (Eastern)
Awadhe, yumi go.	'Uncle, let's go.' (Central/Western)

PRONUNCIATION
Vowels

The vowels in the three Torres Strait Islander languages resemble those of English.

- The simple vowels are:

a	as in 'but'
e	as in 'pet'
i	as in 'bit'
o	as in 'pot'
u	as in 'put'

- The diphthongs are:

ei	as in 'pay'
ai	as in 'bite'
oi	as in 'toy'
au	as in 'now'
eu	pronounced like 'milk' in cockney English

Kala Lagaw Ya has an additional vowel ə (schwa) and semi-vowels y and w. The orthography of the three languages differs when writing the vowel clusters. In Kala Lagaw Ya, i is replaced with a semi-vowel y and u with a semi-vowel w when followed by another vowel. For example, the semi-vowels in KKY dialect are also used as glides which can be inserted in between the vowel cluster ia.

Consonants

All the Torres Strait languages have the consonant sounds: b, d, g, j, k, l, m, n, p, r, s, t, w, y and z, as in English. Kala Lagaw Ya has three additional consonant sounds, dh as in 'the', ng as in 'swing' and th as in 'thin'.

PRONOUNS

	Kala Lagaw Ya	Meriam Mir	TS Broken
I	ngay; ngath	kaka	ai
you	ngi; ngidh; ni (M & K); nidh (M & K)	mama	yu
she	na; nadh	neur	em
he	nuy; nuydh	makrem	em
we (two, exc.)	ngalbe; ngalbay (M & K)	mimi	mitu
we (two, inc.)	ngoeba; ngaba (M & K)	eaka	yumtu
you (two)	ngipel; nipel (M & K)	kiki	yutu
they (two)	palay	gairle	dhemtu

	Kala Lagaw Ya	Meriam Mir	TS Broken
we (exclusive they & I, not you)	ngoey	mimi	mipla
we (inclusive we & I, not you)	ngalpa	mimi	yumpla
you	ngitha; nitha (M & K)	kikiama	yupla
they	thana	gairle	dhempla

GREETINGS & CIVILITIES
Kala Lagaw Ya

How are you?	Ngi midh? (KKY) Ni midhikidh? (M & K)
Fine.	Balabayginga. (KKY) Matha mina. (M & K)
Have you eaten?	Ngi aydu purathima a? (KKY) Ni aydun purthema a? (M) Ni aydun purthema? (K)
I have eaten already.	Ngath aygud mu-asin. (KKY) Ngaw (masc) aygud mina-asin. (M & K) Nguzu (fem) aygud mina-asin. (M & K)
I have not eaten yet.	Ngay aydu purthayginga. (KKY) Ngaw (masc) ayngu purthayginga (M & K) Nguzu (fem) ayngu purthayginga. (M & K)
Come inside the house!	Aya, ngapa lagiya muyari! (KKY) Aye, ngapa mudhiya uth! (M & K)
Thank you.	Eso. (KKY, M & K)
Very good.	Mina boelbayginga. (KKY) Matha mina. (M) Matha mina. (K)

Meriam Mir

How are you?	Nako manali?
Fine.	Sikakanali
Have you eaten?	Aka ma lewer erwe?
I have eaten already.	Kai emethu lewer erwe?
I have not eaten yet.	Ka nole lewer erwe?
Come inside the house!	Ma thaba bau mithem.
Thank you.	Eswau.
Very good.	Dhebe kaine.

Torres Strait Broken

How are you?	Wis wei (yu)?
Fine.	Orait.
Have you eaten?	U bi kaikai?
I have eaten already.	Ai bi pinis kaikai.
I have not eaten yet.	Ai no bi kaikai.
Come inside the house!	Kam insaid hous!
Thank you.	Eso po yu.
Very good.	Prapa gud.

Useful Words & Phrases

	Kala Lagaw Ya	Meriam Mir	TS Broken
Yes.	Wa.	Baru.	Wa.
No.	Lawnga.	Nole.	No.
Welcome.	Sew ngapa.	Maiem.	Maiem.
Goodbye.	Yawa. (KKY)	Yawo.	Siyu; Yawo.
church	Yoewth (KKY)	Zogo metha	Sos
	Maygi mudh (M & K)	Meb	mun
drum	burubur (KKY)	Warup	dram
	warup (M & K)		
God	Augadh (KKY, M & K)	Ople	God
Holy Spirit	Maygi mari (KKY)	Lamar zogo	Oli Gos
	Maygi mar (M & K)		

	Kala Lagaw Ya	Meriam Mir	TS Broken
moon	moelpal (KKY) kisay (M & K)	-	-
priest	misnare (KKY & K) niyay kaz (M)	Bab	pris

DIRECTIONS & THE COUNTRYSIDE

Is that path good?   Able gab debele eki? (MM)
Not so good.   Nole able adud gab eki. (MM)

	Kala Lagaw Ya	Meriam Mir	TS Broken
above	gimal	kotho	antap
behind	kalanu	keubu	biyain
below	apal	sep	andanith
beside	pasinu	meke	klustun
fire	muy	ur	paya
hill	pad	paser	il
in front	parunu	kikem	prant
path	yabugud	kebi gab	rod
left side	boedhadhoegam	kemer pek	lep said
right	gethadoegam	pedike	rait
river	koesa	-riba	-
rock	kula	bakir	ston
smoke	thu	kemur	smok
sun	goeygalim	san	-
tree	puy	lu	tri

PEOPLE & ANIMALS

	Kala Lagaw Ya	Meriam Mir	TS Broken
baby	mapeth (KKY) moekaz (M) moegikaz (K)	kebi werem	beibi
friend	igalayg (KKY) thubudh (M & K)	kimeg	pren

person	mabayg	le	man
man	gargaz (KKY,) garka (M & K)	kimiar	man
old man	kulba thathi (KKY) koey kaz (M & K)	au le	ol man
woman	yoepkaz (KKY) ipika (M & K)	kosker	oman
old woman	kulba apu (KKY) koey kaz (M & K)	au kosker	ol oman
cat	pusi	pusi	pusi
dog	umay	omai	dog
rat	makas	mukeis	rat
snake	thabu (KKY) thab (M & K)	tabo	sneik

FURTHER READING

At present, there's only one publication on Torres Strait Broken. It's in a book called *Broken (Introduction to the Creole Language of the Torres Strait)* by Anna Shnukal, 1988. This is primarily a dictionary, which also contains the grammar of Torres Strait Islander Broken. As for the two indigenous languages of Torres Strait, there are a number of unpublished materials available which can be researched through libraries. There is an article on a sketched grammar, and a short word list on Kalaw Kawa Ya, published in *Languages in Australia*, edited by Suzanne Romaine. The article is by Kevin Ford & Dana Ober, and is called *A Sketch of Kalaw Kawa Ya*.

For more information about Torres Strait Islander culture and lifestyle, see *Torres Strait Islanders: Custom and Colonialism* by Jeremy Beckett (Cambridge University Press, Cambridge, 1987), or the two books by Lindsay Wilson, *Thathilgaw Emereet Lu* and *Kerkar Lu*.

TORRES STRAIT LANGUAGES

TORRES STRAIT LANGUAGES

TEXT

AUSTRALIAN INDEX

ABORIGINAL LANGUAGES INDEX